The Law of the Father?

In *The Law of the Father?* Mary Murray develops a new perspective on the class–patriarchy relationship. Women's rights in and
to property are explored in pre-capitalist and capitalist society.
Exploring the links between kinship, property and patriarchy as
symbiotic and fundamental to the development of the English
state, the relationship between women, property and citizenship
is seen as central to the 'Law of the Father' and the transition to a
'capitalist fraternity'. The book maintains a general link between
property and the legal regulation of sexual behaviour. The author
criticizes the view that women themselves have been property,
arguing that it rests on a historically specific concept of history
projected back in history, where no such concept existed and
reflects changes in ways of thinking about property which
emerged in the course of the transition from feudalism to capitalism.

Mary Murray is Senior Lecturer in Sociology at Massey University.

The Law of the Father?

Patriarchy in the transition from feudalism to capitalism

Mary Murray

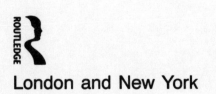

London and New York

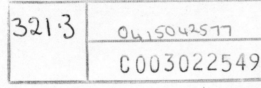
First published 1995
by Routledge
11 New Fetter Lane London EC4P 4EE

Simultaneously published in the USA and Canada
by Routledge
29 West 35th Street, New York NY 10001

© 1995 Mary Murray

Phototypeset in Times by Intype, London

Printed and bound in Great Britain by
Mackays of Chatham PLC, Chatham, Kent

British Library Cataloguing in Publication Data
A catalogue record for this book is available from the British Library.

Library of Congress Cataloging in Publication Data
A catalogue record for this book has been requested

ISBN 0–415–04256–9 (hbk)
ISBN 0–415–04257–7 (pbk)

This book is dedicated with love to my Dad,
George Murray and to my Aunt and Uncle,
Lily and Jack Downes

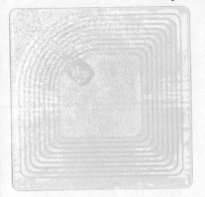

Contents

Acknowledgements

I would like to thank Bridget Fowler, David Frisby, Barbara Littlewood, Derek Sayer and Patrick Wormald for reading and commenting on early draft versions of material now incorporated into this book. Paul Winstanley provided invaluable editorial and moral support and Pat Barnett patiently and persistently typed and retyped several versions of the manuscript. The friendship of Marilyn Barry, Gaynor Graham Te Moana and Anne Marie O'Neill helped me to see the project through to completion. It goes without saying that errors and inadequacies are my own.

Introduction

This book is about a longstanding debate in feminist and social science literature: the relationship between class and patriarchy. For two decades and more, sociologists and feminists have argued about that relationship. Key questions have been: in what way are the two axes of social division related? which, if either, has primacy? what, if any, is the degree of autonomy for each? That debate and the questions addressed within it can be seen as paradigmatic forms of modernist feminist and sociological inquiry and critique. It has been concerned with an analysis of large-scale social inequalities and their causes; and it has been informed by the enlightenment view of the individual subject as capable of questioning truth through reason, and using it to construct an emancipatory politics.

In recent years, particularly since postmodernism has become fashionable in some academic quarters, new, alternative and important questions have been put on the feminist and social science agenda. Indeed the very terms and assumptions of that earlier – structural-modernist – debate have been called into question.

I do not propose to rehearse at length the ins and outs of the postmodernist position. But some of the key arguments in this new current have a bearing on some of the premises and standpoints of this study, and I shall devote a few paragraphs to them here as I think it as well to deal with them before going any further, and in so doing define my own approach.

For some, this new current is seen as one of feminism's greatest challenges.[1] It was Jean-Francois Lyotard's rejection of historical and social meta-narrative that threw down that challenge.[2] Lyotard's chief target was Marxism and its attempt to develop a critique of broad-based relations of inequality around class and property relations. The Marxist conception of society was criticised as reductive, occluding diversity and plurality of social difference. Consequently, attempts to develop critiques of major axes of stratification and domination and subordination, such as gender, class and race, are now seen by many as redundant. We are told that instead of advancing grand social theories we should concern ourselves with more localised, small-scale concrete inquiry, more limited in its aim and sensitive to cultural and historical specificities. The individual subject meanwhile is seen as historically, socially and culturally contingent. The self is not coherent and unified. It is fragmented and plural like the heterogeneous and multifaceted nature of postmodern reality. Notions of truth and justice are similarly seen as contingent and multiple. Indeed, according to Lyotard, we can no longer believe in privileged meta-discourses which transcend local and contingent conditions; emancipatory politics grounded in universal truths are no longer possible.

Postmodern feminism is similarly critical of meta-theoretical accounts of women's oppression. Monocausal analysis of women's subordination, whether liberal, radical, Marxist or psychoanalytic in approach, are eschewed as reductive and dogmatic. They are to be replaced by historically and culturally grounded accounts. Critique of patriarchy as a pervasive axis of domination and subordination is ruled out. Postmodern feminism has also engaged in a re-examination of enlightenment conceptions of the subject, theorising women's identity and subjectivity as multifaceted, complex, fragmented. Resistance to the oppressive structures of class and patriarchal society is to be brought about by the dissolution of the humanist/enlightment subject. This will release her from the regulatory and constraining surveillance imposed by notions of truth and morality.

I do not intend here to rehearse all the analyses and critiques of the postmodern current which have been advanced in recent years. They can easily be followed up within the literature[3] and discussion of them here would only be a red herring within the terms of this book. Again I shall just make a few points which I think are most salient to the assumptions which underpin this study.

In my view the postmodern current can be perfectly well understood within the framework of historical materialism. That view has been advanced by a number of authors including Jameson, Harvey and Callinicos. Jameson theorised postmodernism as the cultural logic of late capitalism.[4] Harvey sees postmodernism as a historical condition, tied to the crisis of accumulation that began in the late 1960s.[5] He, like others, points out that many of the themes of so-called postmodernism were already present in the modernist tradition.[6] For Callinicos the acceptance of post-modernism by the Western intelligentsia is explained by political disillusionment in the aftermath of 1968 and the opportunities for an 'overconsumptionist' life style offered to upper-income white-collar workers since the ascendancy of New Right politics in the West.[7]

In my view patriarchy, like class domination, is multifaceted. A full understanding of it *does* require large-scale social analysis of macro-structures, organisation, institutions and ideology. I see no reason why this should be antithetical to feminist and socio-logical inquiry which is historically, geographically and culturally specific. Either approach can inform the other. Nor does such an analysis automatically fall prey to reductionism. The Marxism advanced in this book is highly critical of reductionism. I shall advance a non-reductive analysis of the class–patriarchy relation-ship within the terms of historical materialism.

Nor does recognition of the complexity of subjectivity have to entail the abandonment of the humanist/enlightenment concep-tion of the subject. The contradictory nature of consciousness is a well-worn theme of much modernist social inquiry, as any stu-dent of gender ideology or class consciousness could illustrate. Those contradictions do not cancel out the goals associated with the humanist/enlightenment subject as an ethical and effective historical agent. Those goals are necessary for feminism if it is to remain an emancipatory movement. The structural debate about class and patriarchy is important for that reason. Positions taken within it inform feminist politics.

As well as the debate about class and patriarchy the book addresses another longstanding lacuna within sociological inquiry. Over the last few decades, historical sociology has become an important new area of scholarship. One of the most important discussions to date in the field has been that which focused on the transition from feudalism to capitalism. That debate of course goes back to the work of Marx, emphasising class conflict,[8] and Max Weber's focus on Protestantism and the spirit of capitalism.[9]

Recent protagonists – Marxist and non-Marxist – have disputed endlessly over the nature and causes of the transition from feudalism to capitalism in Europe.[10]

Postan, an economic historian, focused on the impact of the rise and fall in population levels on landlord–peasant relations. Marxists Sweezey and Wallerstein focus on market and exchange relations as external forces having a disintegrating effect upon feudalism. The Marxist analysis advanced by Maurice Dobb concentrated on the internal contradictions of feudalism which led to its decline, specifically class conflict over feudal exactions by lords from the serfs. Rodney Hilton similarly focuses on class conflict and agrarian transformation. He sees class struggle over rent as the prime mover in the breakdown of feudalism, a struggle internal to the feudal mode of production. American historian and Marxist Robert Brenner's emphasis is also upon class conflict and economic development, stressing the importance of class cohesion and solidarity amongst peasants at village level, as well as the role of the state.

But nowhere in that debate has the issue of patriarchy been examined. The seminal contributions advanced by these 'history men' never considered whether, or to what extent, patriarchal relations were implicated in and or affected by the transition from feudalism to capitalism. Women were for years hidden from history. They have also been hidden from much historical sociology to date.

The structure of this book is as follows. In Chapter 1 I shall consider in some detail the theoretical parameters of the structural debate over class and patriarchy. In Chapter 2 I shall advance my own position regarding the nature of the relationship between class and patriarchy. I shall argue for a *unified systems analysis* of the class–patriarchy relationship. In this context my main focus in the book will be on property. Chapter 3 outlines the main features of feudal society, and key moments in its development. This includes some consideration of the Anglo-Saxon social formation which made an almost spontaneous transition to feudalism, and the impact of the Norman Conquest. I also trace the crisis and breakdown of feudalism from the fourteenth and fifteenth centuries. I then move on to look at the breakthrough of capitalist social relations and outline the main features of capitalist society. Chapter 3 explicates Marxist accounts of the transition from feudalism to capitalism, focusing on the external exchange relations perspective, but more especially on the internal property relations perspective. Towards the end of the chapter I raise some feminist questions about those debates, and signal how I shall look at the relationship between class and patriarchy through an historical analysis of property.

In Chapter 4 I consider patriarchy and rights in and to property. I begin the chapter by looking at material which relates to the Anglo-Saxon situation. More attention is paid though to the post-conquest situation. Finally I consider the implications of the development of the form of property associated with capitalism. Chapter 5 looks at the patriarchal structuring of politics and political power (or its absence), posing the question: to what extent can we characterise the transition from pre-capitalist to capitalist society as a transition from 'The Law of the Father' to 'capitalist fraternity'? Chapter 6 considers the relationship between property and familial relations, concentrating on the extent to which and ways in which we can characterise women's position as equal sisters, but subordinate daughters and wives in Anglo-Saxon, feudal and capitalist society in England. Chapter 7 offers a critical appraisal of feminist contentions that women themselves were property in pre-capitalist England.

My guiding questions will be: what was the relationship between historically specific property forms and women's subordination? and to what extent did the transition from feudalism to capitalism in particular – as expressed in and through changes in property forms – create change and contradiction in patriarchal relations? We shall find that we cannot properly understand either feudalism or capitalism, still less the transition from one to the other, until the patriarchal structuring of property relations is fully perceived.

Chapter 1

The debate

This chapter comprises an analysis of the class–patriarchy debate. The debate dominated much feminist discussion during the 1970s and well into the 1980s. But it has never been satisfactorily resolved. It is a debate which can ultimately only be resolved empirically and historically. The purpose of this chapter however is to outline the *theoretical* debate within which class and patriarchal relations have been analysed.

The structure of the chapter is as follows. Initially, the ways in which theorists have understood the concept of 'patriarchy' will be considered. The chapter will then examine what the various theorists consider to be the root causes of women's oppression. Finally, the extent to which and ways in which the various theorists view the articulation of patriarchal relations with class relations will be analysed. Throughout, it will be demonstrated that the various accounts are fundamentally flawed in both historical and analytical terms.

THE CONCEPT OF PATRIARCHY

In 'The Origins of the Family, Private Property and the State', Engels refers to patriarchy as a form of the family whose essential features were the incorporation of bondsmen, and power vested in the paternal head of the family.[1] Similarly in *The Communist Manifesto* Marx and Engels refer to 'the little workshop of the patriarchal master'.[2] Here patriarchy is understood as a social relation of domestic production.

However, we can see that the definition of patriarchy advanced by Marx and Engels is a limited one. Patriarchy refers to the system under *pre-capitalist* modes of production, in which the means of production and organisation of labour was owned and controlled by the head of household, rather than a more generalised system of female subordination and male domination. Although they certainly did recognise that women were oppressed under capitalism they defined patriarchy at the level of the labour process within pre-capitalist modes of production. Thus in the 'Communist Manifesto' they assert that 'the bourgeoisie, wherever it has got the upper hand, has put an end to all feudal, patriarchal idyllic relations ... and has left remaining no other nexus between man and man than naked self-interest, than callous "cash payment" '.[3]

Although some feminists reject the use of the concept of patriarchy, many, if not most, 'second wave' feminists consider that it gives definition to the nature of women's subordination. Kate Millet, a leading exponent of 'radical' feminism – which brought the concept of patriarchy to the forefront of contemporary feminist debate – in *Sexual Politics* utilises Max Weber's concept of '*Herrschaft*' – a relationship of dominance and subordination – to understand the concept of patriarchy. Patriarchy for Millet refers to the male domination of women, and the domination of younger males by older males. Patriarchal power is thus sex- and age-specific.[4]

Shulamith Firestone, writing in *The Dialectic of Sex*, is the foremost exponent of 'revolutionary feminism' – which developed the radical feminist analysis of the sexual imbalance of power[5] which operates in the interests of men.

Heidi Hartmann, the most influential exponent of the dual systems approach, describes patriarchy in *The Unhappy Marriage of Marxism and Feminism*, as 'a set of social relations between men ... which, though hierarchical, establish or create interdependence and solidarity among men that enable them to dominate women'.[6] Hartmann argues that men, through these relations, derive considerable personal and material benefits, e.g. sexual servicing and a higher standard of living in comparison to women.[7] Christine Delphy, who attempts to develop a materialist feminism in 'The Main Enemy', and whose position is in many ways analogous to that of the dual systems approach, understands patriarchy as a system of exploitation of women by men, through the 'marriage contract', from which men derive considerable material benefits.[8] Similarly, Sylvia Walby who also adopts a dual systems type approach, in *Theorizing Patriarchy* defines patriarchy as 'a system of social structures and practices in which men dominate, oppress and exploit women'.[9]

The concept of patriarchy has also been used by theorists who would classify themselves as Marxist feminists. McDonough and Harrison, for example, in 'Patriarchy and Relations of Production' hold 'a dual notion of patriarchy as, first, the control of women's fertility and sexuality in monogamous marriage and, second, the economic subordination of women through the sexual division of labour (and property)'.[10] Zillah Eisenstein in *Capitalist Patriarchy and the Case for Socialist Feminism* refers to patriarchy as a sexual hierarchy in which the woman is mother, domestic labourer and consumer.[11] Juliet Mitchell, who attempts to develop a Marxist-feminist analysis through the adoption of a neo-Freudian version of psychoanalytic theory, defines patriarchy in *Psychoanalysis and Feminism* as 'the law of the father'.[12] More recently, Michelle Barrett has 'come to regret the aggressive tone of [her] criticisms of this concept . . . and [her] own very limited definition of its appropriate use . . .'.[13] She sees the use of the concept of patriarchy as important for recognising the independent character of women's oppression, to avoid explanations which reduce it to other factors.[14] It will be clear from the ensuing discussion that the extent to which women's oppression is 'independent' from other axes of social division is highly contentious. But I too feel that the concept of patriarchy gives definition to the nature of women's oppression.

We can see, though, from the above by no means exhaustive account of the various definitions of patriarchy that there is no consensus as to the exact meaning of the concept. The discussion in this book is informed by an understanding of patriarchy as involving the economic, political and ideological domination of women by men, which may include but is by no means limited to sexual domination and paternal power. In its paternal form, especially, it is also a form of domination which can be exercised between men.

THE ORIGINS OF PATRIARCHY

It is not my intention in this book to identify the origins of patriarchy. However, I do want to look here at Marxist and some feminist accounts of the origins. The purpose of this is to provide examples of the kind of reasoning that I propose to avoid in this study.

The classic Marxist account of the origins of patriarchy was of course advanced by Engels in 'The Origins of the Family, Private Property and the State'. In short, Engels' thesis was that the position of women was determined by the mode of production; the institution of private property and class society being the crucial factor: 'The first class antagonism which appears in history coincides with the development of the antagonism between man and woman in monogamian marriage, and the first class oppression with that of the female sex by the male. . . .'[15]

Contemporary Marxist feminists McDonough and Harrison consider that 'there remain immense problems surrounding the application and extension of that method to the subordination of women'. However, they argue that 'the way forward for an analysis of patriarchy necessitates an engagement with historical materialism . . . a discussion of the concept of patriarchy in a materialist analysis'.[16] Similarly, Eisenstein attempts 'to formulate socialist feminist questions by using the Marxist method, transformed by feminist commitments'.[17] Patriarchy for Eisenstein 'derives from ideological and political interpretations of biological difference . . . Patriarchal culture is carried over from one historical period to another . . . Material conditions define necessarily ideologies'.[18]

In her attempt to develop a Marxist feminist analysis of the origins of patriarchy – the law of the father – by adopting a neo-Freudian version of psychoanalytic theory, Mitchell agrees with Althusser that psychology is a 'science', the content of which can be annexed to Marxism. Mitchell attempts to root patriarchy in relations of sexual differentiation and power as psychically constituted within the unconscious. According to Mitchell, Lévi-Strauss demonstrated that the biological family was not the distinguishing feature of human kinship structures. Rather, for society to be instituted, the biological base had to be transformed. In this context it is argued that exogamy, as opposed to endogamy, is the essential prerequisite for the inauguration of a cultural kinship system. In short, for humanity to establish itself as it has, certain rules of kinship exchange had to be enacted. In accordance with this, Lévi-Strauss argued that since it is communication and the act of exchange that bind human society together, women became the objects of exchange, representing a sign which is being communicated. Mitchell goes on to argue that such a reading of Lévi-Strauss is consistent with Freud's definition of culture as patriarchal – Freud's work is seen as an analysis *of* patriarchal society, not a recommendation *for* one – as culture is seen as predicated on the symbolic exchange of women by men. Mitchell argues that for Freud the Oedipal moment signifies the entry of man into culture, into everything that made him human. Patriarchy marks the beginning of culture. The 'Oedipus complex' represents the original exogamous incest taboo, the role of the father and the exchange of women and the consequent differentiation between the sexes. The 'Oedipus complex', then, represents the acquisition of sexed subjectivity – the process through which women are subjected to the intersubjective dominance of men. Moreover, Mitchell emphasises that Freud insisted that the 'Oedipus complex' cannot be limited to the nuclear family or the capitalist mode of production. She emphasises that he insisted that the 'Oedipal crisis' was a *universal* event, although its forms of expression vary historically, so that in advanced capitalist societies, its expression occurs within the nuclear family.[19]

Kate Millet feels that preoccupation with the origins of patriarchy can only be speculative. She does, however, argue that 'there is insufficient evidence for the thesis that the present social distinctions of patriarchy (status, role, temperament) are physical in origin'.[20] 'Patriarchy's biological foundations appear to be so very insecure'.[21] Instead, she maintains that there is 'fairly concrete positive evidence of the overwhelmingly *cultural* character of gender'.[22]

According to Shulamith Firestone, the roots of patriarchy are both pre-social and biological. They are pre-social insofar as the oppression of women is 'an oppression which goes back beyond recorded history to the animal kingdom itself'.[23] It is biological insofar as 'the biological family – the vinculum through which the psychology of power can always be smuggled',[24] that is,

> the basic reproductive unit of male/female/infant, in whatever form of social organisation – is characterised by these fundamental – if not immutable – facts:
> 1 That women throughout history before the advent of birth control were at the mercy of their biology – menstruation, menopause, and 'female ills', constant painful childbirth, wet-nursing and care of infants, all of which made them

dependent on males (whether brother, father, husband, lover, or clan, government, community-at-large) for physical survival.

2 That human infants take an even longer time to grow up than animals, and thus are helpless and, for some short period at least, dependent on adults for physical survival.

3 That a basic mother/child interdependency has existed in some form in every society, past or present, and thus has shaped the psychology of every mature female and every infant.

4 That the natural reproductive difference between the sexes led directly to the first division of labour at the origins of class, as well as furnishing the paradigm of caste (discrimination based on biological characteristics).[25]

Although dual systems theorist Heidi Hartmann does not set out to uncover the origins of patriarchy, she nonetheless feels that its basis is material: most fundamental is men's control over women's labour power '. . . the material base of patriarchy . . . does not rest solely on childrearing in the family, but on all the social structures that enable men to control women's labour'.[26] She argues that patriarchal social relations are reproduced in and by the domestic sphere as well as schools, churches, unions, sports clubs, factories, offices, armies, health centres and the media, etc.[27]

Similarly, Christine Delphy, in 'The Main Enemy', argues that the source of patriarchy is the marriage contract, in which the positions of husband and wife are supposedly analogous to that of capital and labour, though the position of the woman in this context is in fact apparently far worse than that of the wage labourer. She argues that the 'marriage contract' is equivalent to the labour contract. Within the 'family mode of production' (autonomous from the capitalist mode of production), we are told that men appropriate women's labour and in so doing constitute their '*class*' of oppressors. Women are thus a class. In return for domestic labour – saving men the expense of purchasing it on the market – we are told that women get only the costs of their own subsistence. She further argues that if women are engaged in waged work, then domestic labour is performed for free.[28] For Walby similarly,

women's household labour is expropriated by their husbands or cohabitees. The woman may receive her maintenance in exchange for her labour, especially when she is not also engaged in waged labour. Housewives are the producing class, while husbands are the expropriating class.[29]

PROBLEMS WITH ACCOUNTS OF THE ORIGINS OF PATRIARCHY

Engels has been frequently criticised, with some justification, for armchair anthropology and conjectural history. These factors may, in part, account for reductionist tendencies in Engels' account: the specificity of *women's* oppression is never fully explored in his theses, nor is the extent to which patriarchal relations may shape class relations.

However, as far as feminist accounts are concerned, as Engels wrote in 'Alexander Jung, Lectures on Modern German Literature', and with obvious contemporary relevance: 'Liberal political principles differed among various personalities, and the position of women gave rise to the most sterile and confused discussions. No one knew where he stood in relation to another person'.[30]

One of the major problems with these feminist accounts is that they work with the same double-edged process of uncritical idealism and empiricism associated with Hegelian philosophy. Discussing this, Marx notes 'the inevitable transformation of the empirical into the speculative and of the speculative into the empirical'.[31] Colletti points out that this entails

> uncritical idealism because Hegel denies the empirical, sensible world and acknowledges true reality only in abstraction, in the Idea. And it is uncritical positivism because Hegel cannot help in the end restoring the empirical object world originally denied ... Hence, the argument is not simply that Hegel is too abstract, but also that his philosophy is crammed with crude and unargued empirical elements, surreptitiously inserted.[32]

In terms of the charge that feminist accounts suffer from uncritical idealism, although Hartmann, for example, seeks to address the material basis of patriarchy, she actually fails to explain why it is that men seemingly control women's labour power. As a result her account is insufficiently materialist, if not implicitly idealist. Similarly, although Mitchell sees that 'Lévi- Strauss suggests there is no theoretical reason why women should not exchange men',[33] she fails to explain why 'empirically this has never taken place in any human society'.[34] Although Millet refers to evidence for the cultural character of gender, she too fails to explain what leads to relations of domination and subordination between men and women.

In this study I do *not* seek or claim to have established the *origins* of women's oppression in England. But in my analysis of the position of women in England historically, I do intend to avoid some of the problems associated with feminist accounts. To do so I will utilise the materialist methodology as outlined by Marx and Engels. This chapter and the next look at various problems in the Marxist analysis of the position of women. Nonetheless in the next chapter I will propose a way of developing a properly gendered Marxism. Here I shall simply outline some important features of the method of analysis advocated by Marx and Engels. Of course in so doing there may well be implications for the origins of women's oppression in England – implications which would ultimately have to be tested by further research.

Marx, though critical of Feuerbach's mechanical materialism,[35] nevertheless utilised Feuerbach's left Hegelian critique of idealism. Basically Marx turned Hegelian dialectical philosophy upside down. Thus, instead of reducing material reality to a predicate of the idea, Marx argued that ideas and consciousness are produced by material reality. In 'The German Ideology' Marx states that:

> Men are the producers of their conceptions, ideas, etc. – real active men, as they are conditioned by a definite development of their productive forces and of the intercourse corresponding to those, up to its furthest forms. Consciousness can never be anything else than conscious existence, and the existence of men, is their actual life process . . . Life is not determined by consciousness, but consciousness by life . . . This method is not devoid of premises. It starts out from the real premises, and does not abandon them for a moment. Its premises are men, not in any fantastic isolation or abstract definition, but in their actual, empirically perceptible process of development under definite conditions. As soon as this active life process is described . . . history ceases to be . . . an imagined activity of imagined subjects, as with the idealists.[36]

According to Marx's premises, the oppression of women cannot be the result of the development of the 'idea' or consciousness as an a priori category. It must be the outcome of concrete historical and material development, requiring a posteriori empirical validation. This study attempts to establish precisely that. It will attempt to demonstrate the ways in which the oppression of women in England has been the outcome of concrete material and historical processes.

In terms of the charge that feminist accounts of the origins of women's oppression suffer from empiricism, a distinguishing feature of empiricism is its attempt to understand the world in terms of given, concrete, *observable appearances*. However, the problem with this is that appearance does not always accord with reality. Marx's analysis of the wage form is instructive in this context. In capitalist societies it appears that wages are equivalent to the amount of work actually done by labourers. But Marx delved beneath this surface appearance and demonstrated that in reality workers are paid the value of their commodity (i.e. labour power), which amounts to the labour-time socially necessary for its production. Capital then appropriates the unpaid surplus labour. Marx demonstrates that the illusions of the wage form derive from the nature of capitalist society, i.e. a society in which the labourer is 'free' of the means of production, and forced to sell her or his labour power as a commodity in order to subsist.[37]

Following this definition of empiricism, insofar as Firestone is a biological reductionist she is also an empiricist. She explains *gender* differences (i.e. social roles), in terms of biological *sex* differences between women and men, rather than in terms of the *social construction of meaning* associated with biological sex differences.

Gerder Lerner, however, in *The Creation of Patriarchy*, though critical of Engels' account of the origins of women's oppression (I shall outline this later), attempts to distinguish 'between biological necessity to which both men and women submitted and adapted, and culturally constructed customs and institutions which forced women into subordinate roles'. She attempts to demonstrate 'how it might have come to pass that women agreed to a sexual division of labour, which would eventually disadvantage them, without having been able to foresee the later consequences'.[38] Indeed she argues for 'the *necessity*, which created the initial division of labour by which women do the mothering'.[39]

Women would choose or prefer those economic activities which could be combined with their mothering duties... the first

sexual division of labour, by which men did the big-game hunting and children and women the small-game hunting and food-
gathering, seems to derive from biological sex differences ...
not differences in the strength and endurance of men and
women but solely reproductive differences, specifically women's
ability to nurse babies.[40]

She discusses the survival of cave paintings and sculptures from
the Neolithic period which seem to suggest that 'women's mothering and nurturing activities, associated with their self-sufficiency
in food-gathering and their sense of competence in many varied
life-essential skills, must have been experienced as a source of
strength, and, probably, magic power.'[41] Lerner stresses that her
own 'acceptance of a "biological explanation" holds only for the
earliest stages of human development ... male dominance is a
historic phenomenon in that it arose out of a biologically determined given situation and became a culturally created and
enforced structure over time'.[42] Although she does not suggest
it,[43] an account such as Lerner's, which does not separate reproduction from social structure, could be encompassed within a
historical materialist account of the origins of women's
oppression.

The empiricist preoccupations of Delphy, too, have been well
demonstrated by the Marxist feminist Maxine Molyneux. Molyneux points out, for example, that Delphy transforms Marxist
concepts into empiricist constructs. Exploitation, for example,
becomes simply appropriation and is not defined at the level of
relations of production. Molyneux notes that even if appropriation does take place, it is not a sufficient basis for the establishment of class: 'some surplus labour is always performed in all
societies on behalf of certain categories of individuals, without
the relations so constituted necessarily being exploitative'.[44] The
concept of class, a universal one in which Delphy places all
women, regardless of differences in wealth and position, thus
loses its specific Marxist meaning.

Similarly, Hartmann's argument that *men* control women's
labour power is empiricist in that it is *merely an impression given
by* bourgeois society. The appearance derives from the separation
of public and private spheres under capitalism. This creates the
illusion that domestic labour is performed for men. Although men
can benefit from domestic labour done by women, the ultimate

beneficiary is capital. Domestic labour performed by women – or in fact men – ensures the daily and generational reproduction of labour power.

But to return to Delphy. Delphy's definition of a mode of production – i.e. her 'family mode of production' – also loses its specific Marxist meaning. A mode of production for Delphy becomes simply a way of producing. In this context Molyneux points out that for Delphy the concept of mode of production becomes 'a descriptive device which sums up her inventory of the characteristic features of housework'.[45]

However, for Marx, a mode of production was defined by *all* social relations necessary to a given mode. In the 'Preface to a Critique of Political Economy', for example, he states: 'the sum total of these relations of production constitutes the economic structure of society'.[46] But Marx does not define the concept of mode of production analytically or *a priori*. Rather, 'Asiatic, ancient, feudal, and bourgeois modes of production can be designated as progressive epochs in the economic formation of society'.[47] This designation is *a posteriori* on empirical grounds. It is worth noting too at this point that despite Molyneux's attempt to marry feminism with Marxism, she too works with a non-Marxist conception of the relations of concepts to data. According to Molyneux, in Marxist discourse the concept of 'mode of production' is an analytical device referring to the social forces and relations of production, and the laws of motion of the particular modes, whilst the conditions of existence of a mode of production, not specified in the general concept, but necessary for its production, refer to a different level of analysis – the social formation. This distinction makes exactly the separations I criticise. It does so insofar as (a) its definition of a mode of production excludes relations of reproduction, shunting them off to a different level of analysis – the social formation; and (b) more generally, it excludes the conditions of existence of a mode of production from its general concept. In 'The German Ideology' relations of production refer to all social relations necessary to a given mode, these being ascertainable only empirically.

It is clear from Marx's historical and empirical analysis of modes of production that relations of production may constitute a much broader totality than normally recognised by base–superstructure models.[48] Marx demonstrates that production relations may comprise 'material', 'superstructural' and even familial relations. In the *Grundrisse*, for example, discussing pastoral and nomadic societies, Marx perceives that 'the family extended as a clan ... appears as a ... *presupposition for the communal appropriation*'.[49] Similarly, in *Capital*, it is clear that Marx does not exclude 'superstructural' elements (in this case 'politics') from the definitions of economic structures. Discussing feudal society Marx drew attention to the fact that surplus extraction was dependent upon the political relation of lordship and servitude.[50] In terms of the capitalist mode of production, whilst Marx demonstrates that the separation of the direct producer from the means of production removes the necessity for direct political coercion, there is a vast literature on the role of the state in the reproduction of capitalist social relations.[51] Similarly, the domestic labour debate has demonstrated the role of the family in the reproduction of the capital–labour relation. I shall return to these points in Chapter 2.

Further, although modes of production may coexist within a social formation during transitional periods, it is necessary to define the *dominant* mode of production to facilitate an analysis of, for example, the state.[52] Delphy's work is also insufficiently *empirical*. Her analysis applies only to certain categories of French women.[53] At the same time, whilst it is possible to perceive ways in which unmarried women are oppressed by marriage, e.g. in terms of the effects of ideological assumptions regarding the proper role for women, not all women's lives are subsumed within the marriage contract.[54]

In her argument that men exploit women within the patriarchal mode of production, Walby[55] attempts to avoid the flaws of Delphy's approach. The attempt is far from convincing. She considers that women as domestic labourers are exploited – they perform more labour but receive less than their husbands. According to that logic, members of the proletariat whose pay and conditions are better than other workers' would constitute a class of exploiters – a clearly nonsensical argument. Are we to assume also that all housewives, regardless of their material circumstance, share a common class position? Walby also considers that domestic labourers are exploited by their husbands because they have no control over the labour power they have produced and over the wage husbands receive from the capitalist exchange. Are we to assume therefore that teachers, for example, are exploited by their pupils because they ultimately have no control over the labour power they help to produce and over the wage pupils eventually receive from the capitalist exchange? Walby also appears to overlook the fact that the 'freedom' of workers (the control they have over their labour power) is a *formal* freedom under capitalism. 'Freedom' from the means of subsistence also means that workers' control over wages is to a large extent a formal freedom.

Mitchell, too, is an empiricist insofar as she adheres to an economistic conception of the mode of production. She differentiates between 'the economic mode of production [and] . . . the ideological mode of reproduction'.[56] Although she does not elaborate her conception of the 'economic mode', to conceive of production in 'economic' terms implicitly commits her to a definition of the mode of production in terms of the *labour process*, rather than in terms of the *social relations* of production. It is the social relations of capitalism, a historically specific form of production, which 'separate' the labour process from other aspects of the mode of production. Similarly, in a critique of Marcuse, Mitchell argues that 'he traps psychoanalysis within Marxist economics . . . this theory retains . . . an economism from Marxism'.[57]

Her account of the origins of patriarchy – the murder of the primeval father – is at the very least questionable. And her account of the operation of 'patriarchy' – the law of the father – is also historically inadequate. Although she argues that patriarchy, located within the unconscious, is expressed in different ideological forms, she actually ignores the historical development of women's oppression and the actual concrete forms it has taken. Although Heidi Hartmann's dual systems thesis fails to analyse sufficiently the extent to which women's oppression has been historically specific, in her use of the concept 'labour power' Hartmann is implicitly committed to an historical analysis, because, as Marx demonstrated, 'labour power' as a historically specific form of labour is integrally related to the capitalist mode of production – a historically specific form of relations of production. It is problematic, then, to view the material basis of patriarchy as men's control over women's labour power in pre-capitalist modes of production.

THE CLASS–PATRIARCHY INTERFACE

Whilst this study does not attempt to establish the *origins* of women's oppression in England, it does attempt to analyse the relationship between class and gender relations across a long period of English history. What follows is an examination of the way in which various theorists have conceived and analysed the relationship between class and gender relations. This will entail consideration of whether or not each of the theorists gives analytic primacy to class or patriarchal relations, the degree of 'autonomy' under which patriarchal relations are said to operate – i.e. to what extent patriarchal relations have an independent dynamic – and conversely, the extent to which the various theorists argue that class and gender relations are interrelated. In so doing I shall attempt to demonstrate the *theoretical* weaknesses which this study aims to avoid.

In both *Women's Estate* and *Psychoanalysis and Feminism*, Mitchell deploys an Althusserian conception of the social formation[58] in an attempt to understand the class–'patriarchy' dynamic. In *Women's Estate*, Mitchell rejects what she considers to be Engels' position, i.e. that the position of women can be derived from the economy. She argues rather that the position of women derives from a specific structure – a unity of various elements. Thus, historically, it will be the outcome of various combinations of elements, i.e. production, reproduction, sexuality and socialization. She further argues that, within the totality, each level has a certain autonomy, though it is ultimately determined by the economic level. Thus contradictions may either negate or reinforce one another. The parameters of the autonomy she sees as determined by dependence on the economy in the 'last instance', i.e. 'because the unity of woman's condition at any time is in this way the product of several structures, moving at different paces, it is always "overdetermined" '.[59]

In *Psychoanalysis and Feminism*, Mitchell attempts to examine the dynamic of sex oppression throughout history. She argues that there is no basic contradiction internal to patriarchy itself, but only as it relates to the social relations with which it is articulated, namely the nuclear family and the organisation of production. However, we are told that

> men enter into the class dominated structures of history, while women (as women, whatever their actual work in production)

remain identified by the kinship pattern of organisation...
harnessed into the family... in such a way that that is where
she will stay. Differences of class, historical epoch, specific
social situations alter the expression of femininity; but in
relation to the law of the father women's position is a compar-
able one.[60]

She argues that patriarchy is a trans-historical phenomenon which
is not simply relatively autonomous, but wholly autonomous:

Though of course ideology and a given mode of production
are interdependent, one cannot be reduced to the other, nor
can the same laws be found to govern one as govern the other.
To put the matter schematically, in analysing contemporary
capitalist society, we are dealing (as elsewhere) with two autonomous areas: the economic mode of capitalism and the ideological mode of patriarchy. The interdependence between them
is found in the particular expression of patriarchal ideology –
in this case the kinship pattern that defines patriarchy is forced
into the straightjacket of the nuclear family. But if we analyse
the economic mode and the ideological situation only at the
point of their interpenetration, we shall never see the means
to their transformation.[61]

Also discussing the relationship between class and patriarchal
relations, McDonough and Harrison argue that

although as Marxists it is essential for us to give analytic primacy to the sphere of production, as feminists it is equally
essential to hold on to a concept such as the relations of human
reproduction in order to understand the specific nature of
women's oppression.[62]

Similarly, Eisenstein writes: 'The ... dynamic of power involved ... derives from both the class relations of production and
the sexual hierarchical relations of society'.[63]

Discussing the relationship between class and patriarchy, as
well as the issue of analytic primacy, Firestone argues that Engels
had a strictly *economic* definition of historical materialism, quot-
ing him from *Socialism, Utopian or Scientific:* 'Historical materialism is that view of the course of history which seeks the ultimate
cause and great moving power of all historic events in the economic development of society'.[64] She nevertheless proposes that

we consider the class–patriarchy relationship by utilising Marx and Engels' dialectical and materialist analytical method. Though, as she perceives, there is a 'whole sexual substratum of the historical dialectic',[65] she proposes a *revised* historical and materialist dialectic. In so doing, she substitutes sex for class as the prime mover in an historical and materialist analysis of history. Citing Engels that 'it is the law of the division of labour that lies at the basis of the division into classes',[66] and utilising his observation that the original division of labour was between man and woman for the purpose of childrearing – that within the family the husband was the owner, the wife the means of production, the children the labour, and that reproduction of the human species was an important economic system in itself[67] – she goes on to rephrase, or rather parody Engels. She argues that:

All past history ... was the history of class struggle. These warring classes of society are always the product of modes of organisation of the biological family unit for the reproduction of the species, as well as the exchange of goods and services. The sexual reproductive organisation of society always furnishes the real basis, starting from which we can alone work out the ultimate explanation of the whole *superstructure* (my emphasis) of economic, juridical and political institutions as well as the religious, philosophical and other ideas of a given historical period.[68]

She also argues that:

Historical materialism is that view of the course of history which seeks the ultimate cause and the great moving power of all historical event in the *dialectic of sex* (my emphasis) the division of society into two distinct biological classes for procreative reproduction and the struggles of these classes with one another, in the changes in the modes of marriage, reproduction and childcare created by these other physically differentiated classes (castes); and in the first division of labour based on sex which developed into the (economic and cultural) class system. And here is the cultural *superstructure* (my emphasis) as well as the economic one, traced not just back to economic class, but all the way back to sex.[69]

In terms of the historical erosion of patriarchal relations, Firestone argues:

So that just as to assure elimination of economic classes requires the revolt of the underclass (the proletariat) and, in a temporary dictatorship, their seizure of the means of *production*, so to assure the elimination of sexual classes requires the revolt of the underclass (women) and the seizure of control of *reproduction*: not only the full restoration to women of ownership of their own bodies, but also their (temporary) seizure of control of human fertility ... so the end goal of feminist revolution must be, unlike that of the first feminist movement, not just the elimination of the male *privilege* but of the sex *distinction* itself: genital differences between human beings would no longer matter culturally ... The division of labour would be ended by the elimination of labour altogether (through cybernetics). The tyranny of the biological family would be broken.[70]

It is clear, then, that in attempting to analyse the relationship between class and patriarchy, Firestone is working with a base–superstructure model of social relations.

Also on the theme of the class–patriarchy interface, according to Millet patriarchy 'run(s) through all other political, social or economic forms, whether of caste or class, feudality or bureaucracy',[71] and 'the fate of three patriarchal institutions, the family, society, and the state are interrelated',[72] and indeed, 'one of the chief effects of class within patriarchy is to set one woman against another'.[73] However, she also contends that class differences between women are transitory and illusory. 'Whatever the class of her birth and education, the female has fewer permanent class associations than does the male. Economic dependency renders her affiliations with any class a tangential, vicarious and temporal matter'.[74] 'Women have ... less of an investment in the class system.'[75] 'It is in the area of class that the *caste*-like status of the female within patriarchy is most liable to confusion, for sexual status often operates in a superficially confusing way within the variable of class'.[76] Thus patriarchy penetrates class divisions, it is all-pervasive, and its analysis is irreducible to Marxist categories.

Although recommending a tactical divorce between Marxism and feminism because of their 'unhappy marriage', in order to understand the class–patriarchy interface Heidi Hartmann does in fact propose that we construct a theory to account for the workings of both patriarchy and capitalism in which both Marxism and feminism are equal partners. She argues that this form of analysis would be most appropriate as patriarchy and capitalism are interrelated, i.e. two interlocking sets of social relations with a joint historical articulation. In fact she argues that a 'partnership' exists between patriarchy and class, such that 'both hierarchy and interdependence among men and the subordination of women are integral to the functioning of our society, i.e. these relations are systematic'[77] and 'the same features, such as the division of labour, often reinforce both patriarchy and capitalism in a thoroughly patriarchal-capitalist society, [so that] it is hard to isolate the mechanisms of patriarchy'.[78] Indeed,

> patriarchy, by establishing and legitimating hierarchy among men (by allowing men of all groups to control at least some women), reinforces capitalist control and capitalist values shape the definition of patriarchal good ... The characteristics of men as radical feminists describe them, competitive, rationalistic, dominating – they are much like our description of the dominant values of capitalist society.[79]

Although she thinks that the partnership between patriarchy and class was not inevitable, as men and capital often have opposing interests, especially over the use of women's labour power, and indeed that 'capital ... encounters pre-existing social forms and ... destroys them',[80] she argues in fact that 'capital is not all powerful'.[81] Patriarchy adjusts to capital and capital adjusts to patriarchy. In this context she further suggests that we investigate 'the contradictions of the patriarchal system ... and their relation to the contradictions of capitalism'.[82]

However, Hartmann further argues that patriarchy and capitalism are conceptually independent, that they are *separate and semi-autonomous* systems such that the sexual division has an *independent* dynamic. We are told in fact that gender has *primacy* over class, i.e. 'capitalist relations of oppression ... [with] ... underlying supports in patriarchal relations of oppression'.[83] Indeed there 'is no necessary connection between the changes in one aspect of production ... and changes in the other'.[84] In fact she thinks that there is little evidence that capitalism is eroding patriarchy. 'We do not think that the patriarchal relations embodied in the family can be destroyed so easily by capital, and we see little evidence that the family system is presently disintegrating'.[85] She asks 'Can we speak of the laws of motion of a patriarchal system?'.[86]

Christine Delphy, given that she perceives that patriarchy has its roots in an *autonomous* domestic mode of production, proposes that we understand the class–patriarchy relationship by recognising that we live in a society made up of two existing modes of production, i.e. the two dynamics which exist and reproduce *independently* of one another. Thus she argues that feminism modifies Marxism because the struggle between labour and capital can no longer be seen as the unique dynamic of society, and Marxist concepts applicable to *male* workers cannot be applied to the oppression of women, as women have different relations to production.[87] For Sylvia Walby, although class and gender affect each other, they 'have independent historical dynamics'.[88]

PROBLEMS WITH CONCEPTUALISATIONS OF THE CLASS–PATRIARCHY RELATIONSHIP

What I want to do now is to demonstrate that the above theorists, in their conceptualisation of the class–patriarchy relationship, work with a 'billiard ball' model of causation, implying atomism, i.e. separate entities, contingently rather than internally related.[89] By a 'billiard ball' model of causation I mean this: in playing billiards, using the cue you cause the cue ball to strike the object ball, which may in turn strike other balls causing movements in various directions. Those particular movements are *contingent* upon the force and angle and impact between the balls. However, there is no *necessity* about one ball striking another. There is no necessity about the particular outcome – it is logically possible that things could turn out differently. And nothing in the *concept* of one billiard ball entails anything about its relation to other billiard balls.

It will also be demonstrated that the theorists cited above reproduce the base–superstructure metaphor which has been associated with crude reductionist/ economistic versions of Marxism which this study seeks to avoid.

In terms of Mitchell's discussion of the class–patriarchy relation, for example, in *Psychoanalysis and Feminism*, McDonough and Harrison point out that

Mitchell's attempt to specify a set of general, abstract, formal propositions about the nature of the unconscious and ideology is theoretically incompatible with a concrete understanding of the forms and conditions and affectivity under which ideology operates and of their relation to other structures within the wider social totality. This disjuncture between immutable forms and historically variant specific contents – the distinction made between the abstract and the concrete – which underpins her analysis is untenable both because these things are conceptualised at different levels of abstraction and there is therefore no homology between the concepts and that to which they allude.[90]

The result is a separation of structures rather than a dialectical integration. Throughout her analysis Mitchell fails to elucidate the relationship between class and women's oppression. She separates the two and attributes to each its own inner logic and dynamic.

Moreover, in *Women's Estate* Mitchell is committed to a base–superstructure model insofar as she argues that the economic level remains primary. Indeed, any commitments she may have to a dialectical understanding of history are rhetorical, as the determinants of the dialectic are known *a priori*. Marx did not formulate dialectical laws of history, Marxism is not a historicism. However, this is certainly the implication of Mitchell's position and, by arguing that the structure of women's oppression is 'overdetermined', the same implication applies for feminism. Moveover, to dictate *theoretically* that the structure of women's oppression is 'overdetermined' implies a mystical interpretation of the Marxist dialectic, rather than a dialectic dependent on *a posteriori* empirical validation.[91]

It is worth noting too that, despite their criticism of Mitchell, in arguing that Marxists should give analytic primacy to production and that feminists should hold onto a concept of the relation of human production, McDonough and Harrison do not actually resolve the problem of the separation of structures themselves.[92] Similarly, for Eisenstein, society is composed of two structures – the capitalist labour process and a patriarchal sexual hierarchy.[93]

Similar pitfalls and weaknesses bedevil Firestone's position. By arguing that the basis of society's superstructure is sexual-reproductive organisation, Firestone substitutes sexual determinism for the supposed economic determinism of Marx and Engels.

Problems associated with the base–superstructure metaphor have already been discussed in relation to Delphy's understanding of the concept of 'mode of production'. These problems will be discussed in more depth later. In the meantime, in terms of Firestone's proposed method of facilitating the transcendence of women's oppression, i.e. the seizure of the means of reproduction, and technological innovation, this fails to grasp the ways in which reproduction and technological innovation are integrally bound up with the wider dimensions of a society's power structure. An implication of Firestone's position is in fact dichotomy.

In terms of Millet's position on the relationship between class and patriarchy, by arguing that patriarchy ultimately transcends class divisions Millet is implicitly committed to a position which suggests that patriarchy is analytically independent of any mode of production. Even if this analytical independence is not meant to be a mimetic model of the real world, but a conceptual *means to* its understanding – it might be possible to conceive of 'pure patriarchy' as an ideal-typical social formation, and consider how, if left to its own devices, it would behave – even Max Weber recognised that ideal-typical social formations are invariably a mixture of elements.[94] This would imply that historically and empirically 'pure patriarchy', existing independently of modes of production, has never existed.

By arguing that capitalism has its underlying support in patriarchy, Hartmann may ultimately have committed herself to a base–superstructure model of society. She is certainly confused in her analysis of the relationship between capitalism and 'patriarchy'. She argues that 'pure patriarchy' does not exist, but also raises the question as to whether or not the patriarchal system has laws of motion.[95]

Sylvia Walby considers that 'The specification of several rather than simply one base is necessary in order to avoid reductionism'.[96] For her

> Patriarchy is composed of six structures: the patriarchal mode of production, patriarchal relations in paid work, patriarchal relations in the state, male violence, patriarchal relations in sexuality and patriarchal relations in cultural institutions.[97]

Ironically, however, by separating mode of production from other levels of the social structure in this manner, she lapses into the economistic definition of relations of production which have characterised base–superstructure models.

Molyneux has drawn attention to the ambivalence of Delphy's thesis. To elaborate – the separation of a 'domestic mode of production' from the capitalist mode of production is not possible, insofar as family subsistence comes from earned income within the capitalist sector, and the performance of domestic labour depends on using and transforming commodities produced and purchased in the capitalist sector.[98] Similarly, if capitalism 'erects family duties as a pretext to exploiting women in their outside work',[99] the separation and autonomy of the domestic mode of production is once again suspect.[100] Indeed, Molyneux points out that it is not possible for a domestic mode of production to exist separately from the capitalist mode of production as housework does not fulfil the criteria which would allow us to conceptualise it as a criterion of periodisation and as a concept upon which our knowledge of determinate social formations depends.[101] It would seem, then, that Delphy's conception of two autonomous modes of production, implying the 'billiard ball' model of causation, is not tenable and, given Walby's statement that 'patriarchy changes but it does not have an intrinsic evolutionary mechanism',[102] it is difficult to see how Walby can also sustain her claim that class and gender have independent historical dynamics.[103]

To sum up: it is my belief that the concept of patriarchy should be used to give definition to the nature of women's oppression. A *broad* definition of patriarchy as the economic, political, sexual and ideological domination of women by men enables us to do this. This study will not concern itself with the origins of patri-archy. My discussion of accounts of the origins was intended to highlight pitfalls which I hope to avoid in my method of analysis, namely reductionism, economism, idealism and empiricism. In the discussion of conceptualizations of the class–patriarchy relationship I argued that atomistic, dualistic and base–superstruc-ture models have dominated the debate. Such models prevent us from grasping fully both the complexity of patriarchal relations and patriarchy as a set of *embedded* social relations. In the next chapter I shall advance my own position on the nature of the class–patriarchy relationship. Because I intend to analyse that relationship historically, I shall also provide working definitions of feudalism and capitalism, outlining different phases in the development of each type of society, paying particular attention to England.

Chapter 2

A way forward

THE CLASS–PATRIARCHY RELATIONSHIP

In this book I intend to develop a *unified system* analysis of the class–patriarchy relationship. I shall analyse class and patriarchy as part of a single historical process. I shall begin with what I believe was Marx's perception of social reality. For Marx, social reality was a complex network of internal relations, single elements which are only what they are by virtue of their relationship to other elements.[1] For example, neither wage labour nor capital can be defined without reference to each other. The existence of a class of wage labourers can only be understood by reference to a class of capitalists; the social categories of wage labour and capital actually imply each other. It will be my argument that the class–patriarchy relationship for the period of English history covered in this study was of this kind: that the social relationships of class and patriarchy contained each other; that neither would have taken the form it did without the other; that it is impossible to understand class or patriarchy during this period as independent, atomistic entities related only contingently; that class and patriarchy were integral parts of a *single* historical process. Once this is grasped, it should become clear that questions about primacy and autonomy – questions which have dogged the structural debate about class and patriarchy – are in fact misplaced. An internal relations perspective is very different from 'traditional historical materialism' – a version of Marxism which has been adopted by many since the Second International.[2] In my view, this version of historical materialism – already widely confuted on various other grounds – also fails when Marxism's potential to become a gendered system of analysis is recognised.

It is a version which rests on a specific reading (a misreading, I would argue) of the 1859 'Preface to a Critique of Political Economy.'

> In the social production of their life, men enter into definite relations that are indispensable and independent of their will, relations of production which correspond to a definite stage of development of their material productive forces. The sum total of these relations of production constitutes the economic structure of society, the real foundation, on which rises a legal and political superstructure and to which correspond definite forms of social consciousness. The mode of production of material life conditions the social, political and intellectual life process in general. It is not the consciousness of men that determines their being, but, on the contrary, their social being that determines their consciousness. At a certain stage of their development, the material productive forces of society come in conflict with the existing relations of production, or – what is but a legal expression for the same thing – with the property relations within which they have been at work hitherto. From forms of development of the productive forces these relations turn into their fetters. Then begins an epoch of social revolution. With the change of the economic foundation the entire immense superstructure is more or less rapidly transformed. In considering such transformations a distinction should always be made between the material transformation of the economic conditions of production, which can be determined with the precision of natural science, and the legal, political, religious, aesthetic or philosophic – in short, ideological forms in which men become conscious of this conflict and fight it out.[3]

Many Marxists – traditional historical materialists – have read this literally: base and superstructure are seen as different component parts of social reality; the base is consigned to the 'economy' or sphere of production whilst the superstructure is interpreted as everything else – politics, art, ideology, the family, etc. Within this version of historical materialism, the base – the economy or sphere of production – is the determining factor in social change: changes in the base are said to determine changes in the superstructure. Even where Marxists attempt to eschew such rigid determinism – Althusser, for example, argued that the superstructure had a degree of 'autonomy' from the economy which was seen as determinate only in the 'last instance'[4] base and super-structure still in fact refer to different and mutually exclusive facets of social reality.

The ontology of an internal relations perspective, however, is very different from the atomistic ontology implied by both 'traditional historical materialism' and 'relative autonomy' models. From the point of view of an 'internal relations' perspective, the concept, and categories of social reality are not *accidentally* or *contingently* related: they are, crucially, *organically* related. Concepts and the social categories to which they refer contain one another. We cannot draw rigid boundaries around them.[5] A quote from Marx illustrates this:

> the simplest economic category presupposes population, moreover a population producing in specific relations, as well as a certain kind of family, or commune, or state etc. It can never exist other than as an abstract one-sided relation within an already given, concrete, living whole.[6]

Marx criticises economists for interpreting the statement that 'every form of production creates its own legal relations, forms of government, etc.',[7] as a causal claim about the relationship between separate entities, and thus treating the relationship as an external, contingent one: 'In bringing things which are *organically* connected into an accidental relation, into a merely reflective connection, they display their crudity and lack of conceptual understanding'.[8] From an internal relations perspective, sociological concepts and categories contain each other. Thus the 'base' actually implies and shapes the 'superstructure' whilst the 'superstructure' actually implies and shapes the 'base'. Base and superstructure are not separate facets of reality at all, they are organically connected.

Marx's discussion of pre-capitalist socio-economic formations in the *Grundrisse* illustrates this well. Discussing pastoral and nomadic societies, for example, he points out that 'family extended as a clan... appears as a... presupposition for the communal appropriation...',[9] meaning that production was organised through the family systems. Similarly, in *Capital*, it is clear that Marx does not exclude 'superstructural' elements such as 'politics' from the definition of economic structures. In feudal society, 'the actual worker remains the possessor of the means of production... the surplus labour for the nominal land owner...

can only be extorted by extra economic compulsion . . .', and thus
'. . . the property relationship must simultaneously appear as a
direct relation of lordship and servitude . . .'.[10] As far as the capitalist mode of production is concerned, the separation of the
direct producer from the means of production has removed
the necessity for direct political coercion. However, political and
legal institutions – superstructural relations par excellence –
remain central to the definition of capitalist relations of production. By this I do not mean that the state is involved simply
in the *reproduction* of capitalist social relations (a point on which
there is a vast literature).[11] More fundamentally, I mean that
capitalism actually *depends* for its existence on political and legal
relations. Historically, property law and legislation regulating
trade union activity have illustrated this well. Enclosure Acts,
for example, ensured the basis for the development of agrarian
capitalism. Later the outlawing of trade unions consolidated the
power of capital over labour. In more recent times the state has
provided important infrastructure services for capital through the
nationalisation of transport, coal, electricity, gas and water. However, we must not lose sight of the fact that the state also assumes
the forms and activities that it does in capitalist society *because*
of capitalist social relations of production. Enclosure Acts, Combination Acts and nationalisation of services would be inconceiv-
able in, for example, nomadic hunting and gathering societies. In
fact I would argue that the state in capitalist society is a particular
form of the social relations of production: the state is *itself* a
relation of production.

What has all this got to do with the relationship between
patriarchy and class? It is my view that the patriarchy–class
relationship is not of the base–superstructure kind. I reject the
crude Marxist view that class structures cause patriarchal structures. I also reject the feminist view that patriarchy constitutes
the base out of which class structures, comprising in effect the
superstructure, emerge. In both of these formulations class and
patriarchy are ultimately seen as separate pieces of social reality.
The same applies to theories which, in an attempt to overcome
the reductionist tendencies of a base–superstructure model, argue
that patriarchy is relatively autonomous. Patriarchy and class, in
such theories, still refer to separate entities.

From an internal relations perspective, patriarchy and class
are not atomistic entities only contingently related, but are

organically connected. It will be my argument that, certainly for the period of English history under consideration in this book, we cannot draw hard-and-fast boundaries around the social relations of class and patriarchy. I shall argue that 'class' actually implied and shaped 'patriarchy' and that 'patriarchy' implied and shaped 'class'; indeed that class relations in English history have been patriarchal and that patriarchal relations have been 'classed'. Class and patriarchy were not separate pieces of social reality at all. They were inseparable.

An analysis of property enables us to perceive the symbiotic relationship between class and patriarchy. For Marx, property lay at the heart of an analysis of social divisions: 'with the division of labour ... is given simultaneously the *distribution*, and indeed the *unequal* distribution, both quantitative and qualitative, of labour and its products, hence property'. For Marx '*division of labour* and private property are ... *identical expressions*: in the one the same thing is affirmed with reference to activity as is affirmed in the other with reference to the product of the activity'.[12]

Following Marx, it is my view that property lies at the heart of an analysis of social divisions. I therefore intend to examine the class–patriarchy axis of social division through an analysis of property. I will demonstrate that for the period of English history analysed in this book we cannot understand patriarchy without reference to property and class, that we cannot understand class without reference to patriarchy and property, nor property without reference to patriarchy and class. This conceptual intricacy demands an internal relations perspective and the dialectical ontology which is central to such a perspective.

Like other feminists I have long been interested in the historical analysis of patriarchy. Millet observes how 'patriarchy exhibits great variety in history and locale'.[13] Similarly, for Firestone there have been 'many different forms of the patriarchal family throughout history'.[14] Hartmann refers to the initiation of patriarchy in state societies and the shift 'from family-based to industrially-based patriarchy'.[15] For Marxist feminists McDonough and Harrison, the precise form of patriarchy is shaped historically by modes of production.[16] For Eisenstein, 'All history may be patriarchal, but this does not mean that the difference between historical periods is not important. It is the specifics which elucidate the general meaning of patriarchal existence'.[17] Meanwhile

Mitchell argues that the Oedipus complex 'can certainly not be limited to the capitalist mode of production', but, she continues, 'this does not amount to saying that it does not assume particular forms of expression under different economic social systems'.[18]

However, the claim that the form of women's oppression has varied historically remains in these accounts little more than an assertion. Within each of these accounts there is little if any systematic attempt to analyse different types of gender subordination historically. In recent years, however, feminist historians have begun to undertake such work. But most historians – feminists included – tend to fight shy of advancing theoretically informed, overarching, epochal forms of historical analysis. Such an approach has more usually been the terrain of sociologists. But even historical sociologists, as I have already indicated, have invariably failed to marry this approach with feminist questions. As a feminist sociologist, Sylvia Walby, however, has made the attempt to periodise patriarchy. Walby sees that, 'The rise of capitalism transformed class relations, changing the very classes which constituted society', but feels that:

> This historical shift did not have such dramatic effects upon gender relations... only a minor shift in the relative significance of public and private sites of patriarchy occurred. The trajectory towards an intensified private form of patriarchy, which can be identified as far back as the seventeenth century... accelerated.[19]

It will be a central thesis of mine, however, that the rise of capitalism *did* have dramatic effects upon patriarchy. I shall argue that it did so because the meaning and definition of property changed with the development of capitalism, and because patriarchy was intrinsic to the constitution of pre-capitalist property forms. The transition could not then avoid changing the nature of patriarchy. Walby's failure to grasp this arises from her dualistic formulation of the patriarchy–class relationship. She feels that a developed concept of patriarchy is the best way of theorising any changes that did occur.[20] Now although we can develop the concept of patriarchy so as to encompass its different forms – e.g. feudal patriarchy and capitalist patriarchy – it is my contention that of necessity this would entail an analysis of historical shifts and changes in property and class relations. It is my intention in this study to analyse gender relations at different historical junctures, elucidating the way in which women's oppression has been related to different forms of property relations in England, paying particular attention to feudal and capitalist forms of property.

FEUDALISM AND CAPITALISM

Feudalism

The first phase in the development of feudal society occurred between the collapse of the West Roman Empire and the tenth century. During this period, barbarian successor states replaced the collapsed political system of the Romans.[21] The Romans had departed the shores of England by the mid-fifth century. Invasions of England by the Germanic barbarian tribes which began in the fourth century continued into the sixth century.[22] Barbarian societies were far from primitive, having a division of labour differentiated beyond that of age and sex to include full-time craft specialists, priests and traders, and emergent classes.[23]

Whilst kinship remained an important organising principle of Anglo-Saxon society, by the seventh and eighth centuries consolidated social hierarchies had evolved.[24] A feudal economy was gradually emerging from within the barbarian states. We can see this clearly in England where social classes included kings, lords, peasants and slaves. Even as late as the eleventh century slaves still existed in considerable numbers.[25] After the Germanic invasions there was a general tendency towards more and more rural dependency amongst the peasantry.[26] By the seventh century the hide, a measure of land and tribal resource, had become a unit of exploitation by lords. According to the laws of the West Saxon King Ine, the hide was a unit of land associated with the basic status of freeman. It was supplied to him as of right by the wider kin group. This freeman might be a lord in his own right, using labour from outside the nuclear family to work the land. Indeed, due to the loosening of ties between wealth and status, many peasants, while legally free, were the tenants of manorial lords.[27] In this vein, Whitelock notes 'by about 700, and perhaps long before, there were men who took their land at a rent from a lord, and, if they also accepted a homestead from him, he had a right to agricultural services as well as rent'.[28]

T. M. Charles Edwards suggests that 'the hide was the unit of land which bound together in one coherent system the lineage, the hierarchy of status and also, perhaps, the relationship of lord and vassal'.[29] One's lord may very well have been the head of one's kin group. In Anglo-Saxon society a holding of five hides could give a man the status of lord.

> If a ceorl [the lowest rank of freeman] prospered, so that he possessed fully five hides of land of his own, a bell and a castle-gate, a seat and a special office in the king's hall, then was he henceforth entitled to the right of a thegn.[30]

At the turn of the seventh century a hereditary and legally defined aristocracy of thegns was consolidated.[31] Exploiting estates of a proto-manorial type they dominated the rural social structure[32] and provided support for the king.

Over time, the English heptarchy of kingdoms became unified. The tribal hidage was abolished and replaced with the shire, the new administrative unit of the bureaucratic and exploitative state.[33] By the eleventh century the monarchy had an advanced and coordinated administrative system, taxation, currency and justice throughout the country.[34]

Discussing Anglo-Saxon society, Perry Anderson says that, although it was not yet organised into a new and coherent mode of production,[35] 'the Anglo-Saxon social formation that succumbed to the Norman Invasion had been the most highly developed example in Europe of a potentially "spontaneous" transition of a Germanic Society to a feudal social formation'.[36]

We can date the second phase of the development of feudalism from approximately 1000 AD to the early fourteenth century.

> This period saw a marked growth of population, agricultural and manufacturing production and trade, the virtual revival of cities, a great outburst of culture, and a striking expansion of the Western feudal economy in the form of 'crusades' against the Moslems, emigration, colonisation and the setting up of trading-posts abroad.[37]

In England a centralised feudalism was imported from the outside by the Normans and systematically implanted from above.[38] William the Conqueror distributed around 5,000 fiefs to occupy and secure the country. Unlike continental Europe, in England subvassals had to swear allegiance to their immediate lords *and* the monarch, the donor of all land. Pre-feudal survivals such as the fyrd militia and the defence tax – the danegeld – were also used by the Norman kings to strengthen the state. It was the most unified and solidified state in Western Europe at the time. Although manorialism and seigniorial exploitation were not developed to the same degree in all areas of the country, there was a general and definite trend towards the enserfment of the peasantry.[39]

The feudal crisis of the fourteenth and fifteenth centuries marked the third phase of feudalism, and an important period for its breakdown. It was characterised by a collapse of large-scale feudal agriculture, of manufactures and international trade, plagues, population reduction, ideological crisis and social revolution.[40] In England during this period serfdom declined. This phase – often referred to as the 'breakdown' of feudalism – was superseded by a period of renewal and expansion from the mid-fifteenth century through to the mid-seventeenth century.[41]

Historians, in particular non-Marxist historians, have tended to adopt a fairly narrow definition of feudalism, as a specific *relationship within the medieval ruling class*, i.e. a relationship between feudal lords and vassals, with vassals holding land from a feudal overlord in return for military service, attendance at the lord's court and aid and counsel to the lord. Through a system of subinfeudation vassals could themselves become overlords.[42] Sociologists and Marxist historians[43] have tended to adopt a much wider definition of feudalism as a specific *social order*, the form of society in Western Europe from approximately 500 AD to 1500 AD, i.e. from the collapse of the Roman Empire to the early modern period. Although the periodisation here is loose, it is not arbitrary, referring to the rise and fall of similar social formations throughout Western Europe. Although there were differences between those European societies, they shared a number of common features. In each European feudal society peasants were the direct producers. Populations consisted of family groupings growing crops and rearing animals on smallholdings. This involved both subsistence and surplus production; subsistence production provided for the basic needs of the family whilst surplus production provided for those sections of society who did not produce. The existence of surplus extraction relations in feudal societies had important implications: there was a division of labour between producers and non-producers and this division formed the key axis of class division in those societies.

The size of peasant landholdings varied according to climate, demography (fewer peasants in any one place could mean more land for them) and inheritance practices. The upper limit of holdings would be determined by the size of the labour force available to work the land. The labour force of a holding was made up of nuclear family members and, in the case of wealthier peasants, servants. Consequently richer peasants could not expand until the development of a 'free' labour force.

Peasant farms were clustered into villages. The strong collective and communal elements built into the way the land was farmed provided a basis for class consciousness and resistance to lords (a point to which I shall return later). The commonest method of farming in the village was the open field system. Strips of land of varying quality was allocated to families. Decisions about what was grown and when it was grown were made collectively by the village. Peasants also had access to rights of common from which they could gather wood, peat, nuts and fruit, etc. This was very important for the subsistence of poorer peasants (particularly when, as we shall see, landlords began to enclose land). Rights of common were controlled by manorial courts where feudal lords exercised jurisdiction.

Systematic and dramatic inequality existed amongst the peasantry. Serfdom as a personal status emerged following the break-up of the Roman Empire. Many former slaves became serfs and, between the fifth and tenth centuries, many feudal aristocrats forced the free peasantry into serfdom for military purposes. Serfs were tied to the land and were subject to greater surplus extraction by lords than were free peasants.

Amongst the free peasantry a well established group of the better-off had full holdings and full grazing rights. Smallholders, who at Domesday in 1086 comprised a third of the English peasantry, were often unable to support their families from their holdings. They had to supplement their income by working part time, often as seasonal wage labourers. Between the substantial and smallholders there existed a fluctuating band of middle peasantry.

In town and country alike there were numerous craftsmen. Many were itinerant, though in the countryside they often had landholdings. In the towns lords extracted surplus from artisans through rents, tolls and taxes.

Servants, who were basically landless labourers, were always a minority. There were three main groups: permanent employees of lords, such as shepherds and dairymaids, living-in servants in richer peasant households (they were often younger members of other holdings waiting for their own holding), and seasonal wage labourers who, we have already seen, were often smallholders themselves seeking to supplement their income.

Stratification amongst the ruling class was basically threefold. The aristocracy or magnates were few in number and were closely interrelated by family ties. They owned vast stretches of land and dominated feudal politics. The gentry were greater in number but their landholdings were less. Their political importance increased in England with the development of agrarian capitalism. In the towns, merchants, the third grouping, acted as intermediaries between petty producers. They too wielded considerable political power and influence.

Marx saw the relationship between the peasantry and aristocracy and gentry as an exploitative one. He saw feudalism as a specific form of exploitation. That exploitation constituted the basis for the entire social structure. Whereas non-Marxist historians have seen military relationships as the basis for feudalism, Marxist historian Rodney Hilton points out that even in the fifteenth century, long after the decline of military service, the enormous income of the great landed aristocrats was based on rent.[44] For Marxists, the essence of the feudal mode of production was an exploitative relationship between landowners and subordinated peasants, in which surplus beyond subsistence was transferred to the ruling class by coercive sanction. Force or coercion was necessary to ensure the transfer of surplus because the peasantry were in possession of the means of production. The feudal ruling class had no managerial functions as regards the production process. Theoretically, therefore, the peasantry were not dependent upon the ruling class. Because the ruling class were actually superfluous to the production process they had to put ideological pressure of a paternalist nature on the peasantry to ensure the transfer of surplus.

Surplus was in the form of 'rent'. Holding land from lords who acted as their protectors, tenants had to pay rent either in labour, kind (e.g. crops) or money. The forms of rent varied over time and from place to place. Labour rent was by no means the definitive form of rent – commutation to cash or kind did not constitute the breakdown of feudalism.

Serfs were subject to greater surplus extraction; their labour services were heavier. They were also subject to the heriot tax – a death duty through which lords could claim, for example, a dead man's best beast – and a marriage tax, the merchet. Nor did they share the same rights as the free peasantry; they could not buy and sell land, they were unable to move or marry freely and they were tried in manorial rather than royal courts. (In continental Europe but not England, they were subject to *haute justice* – the use of the death penalty by feudal lords.)

Feudal lords also benefited from the profits of jurisdiction. They could impose banalities, e.g. fines, fees and taxes, for such things as the use of the lord's mill, oven or winepress. According to Rodney Hilton, the profits of jurisdiction contributed significantly to surplus extracted from peasants by lords.[45] To understand how this worked we need to understand the political set-up of feudalism. Today, economic, political and legal power are institutionally separated. In feudal society all three powers coincided in particular individuals. Local barons, for example, were landowners exercising political power and jurisdiction. Further, whereas today sovereignty is invested in the nation state, i.e. a single legislative institution with a monopoly of political and judicial power, as Perry Anderson has shown, feudalism was characterised by the parcelisation of sovereignty. Feudal lords other than the king exercised a degree of territorial, political and legal power. Even in England, where the state was much more unified and centralised than in other feudal polities, feudal lords were able to exercise political and legal power over the peasantry. It was this power that enabled them to extract the profits of jurisdiction.

CAPITALISM

The capitalist mode of production has developed at different times in different places. Marx saw England as the classic ground of capitalist development. With agrarian capitalism developing from the sixteenth century, by the middle of the seventeenth century a good deal of the land in England was owned by capitalist farmers who employed wage-labour and produced for a commodity market. Early social differentiation amongst the peasantry, the Reformation and Enclosure Acts had been significant in this process. The Civil War and Revolution of the seventeenth century marked the breakthrough of capitalist society. It was followed by a period of economic expansion. In the eighteenth century, the American Revolution, the French Revolution and the Industrial Revolution in England marked the triumph of the capitalist mode of production.[46]

Referring to the activities of European merchants in the twelfth and thirteenth centuries, Pirenne's definition of capitalism was 'the tendency to the steady accumulation of wealth . . .'.[47] For de Roover the commercial revolution at the end of the thirteenth century paved the way for 'mercantile capitalism, which in most European countries was not replaced by industrial capitalism before the middle of the nineteenth century'.[48] For Max Weber old-style capitalism based on a lust for and ruthless, often violent, acquisition of wealth existed in traditional, economically conservative societies. In 'old-style capitalism' wealth was pursued for personal pleasure or aggrandisement and was not ploughed into productive investment. For Weber this contrasts to modern ascetic capitalism characterised by the lawful, non-violent, sober and rationally calculating pursuit of profit which is ploughed in to productive investment. Weber sees modern capitalism as essentially ascetic, that is self-denying and opposed to pleasure and worldly enjoyment.[49]

Following Marx, however, in this study capitalism will be understood as a *mode of production*. Trade and commerce certainly did exist in feudal society, but feudal society was primarily an agrarian society. The most important social relationship in feudal society was an exploitative and conflictual class relationship between landlords who extracted surplus beyond subsistence from tenants. Capitalism is a system of generalised commodity production. Virtually everything including, crucially, labour power, becomes a commodity bought and sold in the market place. The fundamental social relation of capitalism is a class relationship between capital-owning entrepreneurs and formally 'free' wage labourers (free of the means of production and free to sell their labour power). The relationship between capital and labour is exploitative and conflictual, capitalists extracting surplus labour time/value from the proletariat.[50] For Marx, in the capitalist mode of production as in any other, social and political institutions, ideas and consciousness are an expression of the principal social relationship between labour and capital. What Marx and contemporary Marxists have failed to consider is how that social relationship was constructed through patriarchal relations.

Chapter 3

Marxism and the transition from feudalism to capitalism

In this chapter I shall outline Marxist explanations of the transition from feudalism to capitalism. I will not go into everything that has been said; I shall concentrate on those accounts which are most relevant to the themes of this book. I shall begin by summarising Marx's own account of the transition from feudalism to capitalism, moving on to more recent Marxist views: the 'external' exchange relations perspective, and the 'internal' property relations perspective. My exposition will also include some criticisms of those positions. At the conclusion of the chapter I shall raise some feminist questions about those debates, and outline how I will look at property and patriarchy in Anglo-Saxon society and in the shift from feudalism to capitalism.

MARX

For Marx[1] the basis of capitalism is an exploitative social relation between a property-owning capitalist class and a propertyless class of 'free' wage labourers. He saw this social relation as more fundamental than the profit motive, the extension of the market or the existence of wage labour. By 'free' wage labour Marx meant labour which was 'free' to sell its labour power as a commodity. In contrast to the serf or slave who is 'owned', the 'free' wage labourer can enter into contracts to sell his or her labour power. The labourer is also 'free' of the means of production or subsistence. Basically the worker is propertyless, and therefore *forced* to sell labour power to capital.

Marx sees the creation of 'free' wage labour as a *violent* process. He identifies two processes involved in this. The first was the emancipation of the serfs by the end of the fourteenth century and the breakdown of guild control of wages. Second, the peasantry and petty producers had to be separated from their own means of production. Marx saw the breakdown of peasant independence and their subordination to capital as the secret of the 'primitive' accumulation of capital. He identifies a number of factors which were significant in this process. At the end of the fifteenth century through into the early sixteenth century, feudal lords, impoverished by war and conspicuous consumption of luxuries, hurled a mass of 'free' proletarians into the labour-market through the dissolution of bonds of feudal retainers (i.e. hangers on, attendants and followers). Following the Reformation of the sixteenth century and the nationalisation of the monasteries, numerous monks were in effect made redundant and thrown out into the ranks of the proletariat. Monasteries also ceased to be sanctuaries for those without any other alternatives. Initially the seizure of church land and the establishment of the king as head of the church enhanced the power of the Crown. In the end, however, most of the church land was sold off and ended up in the hands of the gentry. This weakened the financial independence and thus the power of the Crown, and had important consequences for the rise of capitalist agriculture. Enclosure of the land began from the fifteenth century, turning arable land into pasture and forcibly driving the peasantry from the land. Rights of common were also abolished.

Initially turned into vagabonds and beggars, the expropriated peasantry were subjected to force and violence on the part of the state disciplining them for wage labour. Marx discusses in some detail the use of 'bloody legislation against the expropriated'.[2] During the reign of Henry VIII vagabonds could be whipped, imprisoned, perhaps lose half an ear or even be executed for not working. Under Edward VI anyone who refused work could be condemned to slavery. Under an Elizabethan law of 1572, unlicensed beggars were to be severely flogged and branded. For repeated offences they would be executed. Similar punishment was meted out under James I. These statutes remained legally in force until the beginning of the eighteenth century. From the fourteenth century legislation was also used to regulate wages.

Marx then goes on to explain the origin of capitalist farmers. Central to this was the process of social differentiation amongst the peasantry. Over the centuries, changing forms of land tenure had the effect of dividing up the agricultural population into various groups. Under changing economic circumstances and with legal restrictions on land use, some groups were enriched while others were impoverished, until in the sixteenth century rich capitalist farmers emerged.

Emphasising social processes in the countryside, Marx disputed the role of merchant capital as prime mover in the transition from feudalism to capitalism. Merchant capital was located in the sphere of circulation between small producers rather than in the sphere of production. Manufacturing in feudal society was concerned with the production of luxuries. The production process was highly skilled, slow and costly. Guild control kept both the quality and price of luxury commodities up so as to extract as much as possible from lords. All of this was not conducive to capitalism.

For capitalist manufacturing to develop, new industries had to develop in areas outside guild control. Marx saw the colonial system which developed from the late fifteenth century as important for this process. The rapid influx of capital and precious metals from overseas conquests enabled new manufacturers to become established at sea ports and at inland centres outside the control of older corporate towns and guild organisation.

Crucially, however, Marx emphasises that the development of capitalism was dependent upon the creation of labour as a commodity. He sees *agrarian* social relations as the key to this process, a process which involved 'the most shameless violation of the "sacred rights of property" and the grossest acts of violence to persons'.[3]

EXTERNAL MARXIST

Exchange relations perspective

Both Sweezey[4] and Wallerstein[5] define feudalism as a system of production for use, with a relatively low division of labour and limited development of trade. They see capitalism as a system of production for profit which takes place through market exchange. An international trade-based division of labour expresses the expansive nature of the system. Capital accumulation is necessary to the generation of exchange value and capitalism is founded on that fact.

The transition from feudalism to capitalism is explained in

terms of external forces acting upon the feudal system. Conflicts internal to feudalism, such as between town and country or between lords and serfs, are not seen as sufficient to cause the breakdown of feudalism and the emergence of capitalism.

Sweezey emphasises the role of trade and of towns, ranging from short-distance trade in food and manufactured goods to long-distance trade in luxury goods. This created a division of labour between town and country. Thus exchange relations with a dynamic of expansion *external* to feudal 'production for use' caused feudalism to decline.

Wallerstein defines capitalism as a *world system*, rather than a set of social relations of production within nation states. The capitalist world system is expressed through an international division of labour and the universalisation of market exchange relations. For Wallerstein 'capitalism involves not only appropriation of surplus value by an owner from a labourer, but also an appropriation of surplus of the whole world-economy by core areas'.[6] 'Core' nation states benefit from the unequal exchange of commodities with weak 'peripheral' states. Whereas wage labour dominates within the 'core' nation states, various forms of 'unfree' labour may be utilised elsewhere. Consequently, for Wallerstein the most significant fact to be explained is the expansion of the international division of labour rather than the emergence of free wage labour within Europe. However, one of the arguments Wallerstein uses to explain the capitalist world system is the establishment of strong 'core' states in Europe. Nonetheless he explains the emergence of 'core' states in terms of international market forces.

Both Sweezey and Wallerstein have been seen as representing a 'Smithian' form of Marxism.[7] Both authors seem to assume Adam Smith's 'hidden hand' of economic self-interest to explain how an expansive force for capitalist development arose external to feudalism's own logic. They appear to follow Adam Smith's view that there is an inherent tendency in everyone to 'truck, barter and exchange' in pursuit of one's own interests.

Furthermore, as Simon Clarke observes, the market was not in fact external to feudalism, it was actually an aspect of the development of feudal relations of production.[8] Feudalism was not a static system, trade and economic expansion were compatible with that society. Trade, especially international trade, was an integral part of feudalism, important for satisfying the demands of feudal lords for luxury consumption. Medieval towns were feudal foundations rather than centres of proto-capitalist entrepreneurship. Urban merchants were not 'free' burghers intent on establishing the capitalist system. They were in fact parasitic on the feudal order.[9]

Recent studies suggest that 'exchange relations' theorists of the transition have exaggerated the extent to which international trade was of sufficient scale to promote the transition from feudalism to capitalism. Connections between economies and within states were weak, tenuous and likely to be interrupted.[10] It was Marx who was the first to point out that merchant capital could not explain the process of primitive accumulation in England. For Marx merchant capital by itself was incapable 'of promoting and explaining the transition from one mode of production to another'.[11]

INTERNAL PROPERTY RELATIONS PERSPECTIVE

Maurice Dobb, Rodney Hilton and Robert Brenner advance an account of the transition based on the social relations of production, relations which I see as being synonymous with property relations. The capitalist mode of production is defined by wage labour, the commodification of labour power being central to the processes of capital accumulation. The development of trade and commerce and the international division of labour are expressions of different forms of property relations.

Dobb[12] sees the disintegration of feudalism as coming about through an interaction between the external impact of the market and relationships internal to the system. However, he sees internal relationships as the most important. To meet their demands for an increasing revenue supply for warfare and luxury consumption, feudal lords often increased the burden of exactions on serfs. The upshot of this was class conflict through which some serfs were able to win their freedom: serfdom would tend to be retained where labour productivity was low and labour was scarce. An inability to pay wages would act as a brake on the overthrow of serfdom. Wage labour would be viable where labour productivity was high enough and wages low enough for lords to expect a reasonable retention of surplus. Out of this there emerged a complex transitional social structure of peasants and small commodity producers. Further social differentiation within the 'transitional' society resulted in a basic division between the owners and non-owners of capital, i.e. capitalism.

Dobb's emphasis on class conflict and agrarian transformation is shared by Rodney Hilton. Hilton[13] sees class struggle over rent as the prime mover in the breakdown of feudalism. He does not ignore the market as an impetus on lords to increase rent, but this is seen as *internal* to the feudal mode of production. The maintenance and extension of class power in the hands of the ruling class is seen as the driving force in the feudal economy and feudal politics. The ruling class strove to increase feudal rent to maintain and improve their position as rulers against rivals from within their own class. For this reason lords sought to maximise rent. Peasants were also keen to secure surplus for themselves. They were sometimes able to enforce a reduction of rent, or an increase in the productivity of the holding and cultivation of new land. Lords were similarly interested in expanding cultivation. (Hilton argues that the expansion of cultivation until the end of the thirteenth century was therefore a product of rent struggle rather than as Postan, whom I shall consider below argues, due to population pressure.) Economic development was therefore bound up with class struggle in and around rent. Long term, the result was the commutation of labour-rent into money-rent, a switch which Hilton, unlike Dobb, sees as consistent with feudalism because the overall judicial power of feudal lords remained in place. The retention of surplus provided the basis for commodity production and increasing stratification amongst the peasantry. Holton says of Hilton: 'his study of the English peasant revolt of 1381 links the theme of endemic peasant resistance to feudal exactions, with the gradual development of free tenures, and the growth of a social structure differentiated between capitalist and wage-labourer'.[14]

For American historian Robert Brenner,[15]

> It is in the outcome of class conflicts – the reaffirmation of the old *property relations* or their destruction and the consequent establishment of a new structure – that is to be found perhaps the key to ... the transition from feudalism to capitalism [my emphasis].[16]

In advancing his thesis he is critical of Postan's demographic model of the transition and models which stress the role of the market.

Postan, an economic historian, put forward a materialist though non-Marxist explanation of change and development in English feudal society.[17] His framework is essentially Malthusian, analysing cyclical demographic dynamics. Postan's thesis can be broken down into three component parts: land use, population and technology. Regarding land use, Postan argues that until the fourteenth century the amount of land under cultivation was increasing. From the second half of the fourteenth century the area of land under cultivation declined. He sees this pattern as being determined by the rise and fall of population. Until the early fourteenth century population increased. This caused rents and the price of land to increase. By the beginning of the fourteenth century English peasant society was approaching the margins of subsistence. The productivity of the land was falling and the peasantry were near to mass starvation, with increasing numbers of deaths, especially in the years of bad harvests. His argument then is basically that before the first half of the fourteenth century overpopulation was pushing up the death rate. Postan certainly recognises the role of the Black Death (1348) in wiping out a sizeable proportion of the English population, but he argues that population decline occurred before this. The virulence of the Black Death is explained by the undernourishment and weakness of the peasantry. He sees it as merely *aggravating* the mortality rates of the early fourteenth century.

During the first half of the fourteenth century, evidence suggests that the population ceased to expand, indeed that it declined. For Postan the crucial indicators of this are that land values decreased and wages increased.

In Postan's opinion agricultural technology was of significance in the processes he outlines because it did not keep up with increases in population. This meant that economic expansion was lateral, i.e. more and more bad or virginal land was brought under the plough. At the same time increasing amounts of land were cultivated for arable purposes at the expense of pasture. In the absence of artificial fertilisers the result was the exhaustion of land. As land became increasingly infertile agricultural productivity fell. Conversely, when population collapsed during the first half of the fourteenth century the balance between arable and pasture was restored and the fertility of the land increased.

The significance of Postan's argument for the relationship between lords and peasants in English feudal society is this. Population increase determined the strength of feudal lords *vis-à-vis* the peasantry. The increase of population brought a rising demand for food and the peasantry accepted a degradation of their status, i.e. an increase in rents and taxes. Conversely, population decrease increased the strength of the peasantry *vis-à-vis* feudal lords. In line with the laws of supply and demand, population collapse brought a fall in rents, an increase in wages and release for the peasantry from their servile obligations.

Commenting on all of this, Brenner maintains that the Malthusian cycle of long-term stagnation or economic backwardness can only be fully understood as a product of established structures of class relations. He views economic development as the result of new class relations more favourable to new organisations of production, technical innovations and increasing levels of productive investment. More specifically, Brenner draws attention to the fact that the demographic model breaks down in the face of comparative analysis: similar demographic trends in Europe did not result in the same outcomes. For example, in England rising population levels coincided with an increase in the power of feudal lords. In the Paris area at the end of the thirteenth century, however, rising population coincided with the establishment of peasant freedom. Further growth of population leading to rising demand for land would tend to increase the power of lords to extract rent, but only if lords had already successfully established the right to do so. Who gains and who loses from rising population and growing demand for land, bringing higher land prices and rent increases, is actually subject to prior determination by the character of the landlord–peasant class relation.

Brenner also rejects, on historical and comparative grounds, models which privilege the role of the market in the breakdown of feudalism. Areas close to markets did not always undergo a dissolution of serfdom. In Eastern Europe the impact of the market – e.g. the grain trade – actually tightened peasant bondage. He disputes the argument that the growth of towns can account for the collapse of serfdom in the west by 1500. Towns were not big enough, nor were there enough of them to attract the rural masses. In any case there were few runaway serfs with sufficient capital or skill to enter the ranks of the urban population. Moreover the urban ruling class allied with the nobility against the peasantry. The urban ruling class were themselves often landowners and in common with the rural ruling class they had an interest in exploiting serfs to facilitate exchange.

Brenner's own explanation of the decline of serfdom and the emergence of agrarian capitalism centres on class conflict and economic development. In terms of the decline of serfdom we have seen already that Brenner disputes the demographic crisis as a natural fact. He sees it as built into peasant organisation of production and the social relationship of serfdom, within which surplus extraction acted as a barrier to mobility. To elaborate: Brenner points out that surplus extracted by lords was not ploughed into productive investment. Most of it was squandered in military expenditure and conspicuous consumption. Moreover, the most obvious way for lords to increase their income was not through capital investment and new techniques, but through squeezing the peasantry. Because of surplus extraction by lords and maldistribution of land, peasants were unable to use the land in a free and rational manner. Unable to put back into the land what was taken out of it, the surplus extraction relations of serfdom tended to lead to the exhaustion of peasant production. Brenner sees this crisis of productivity, bound up with feudal class relations, as leading to demographic crisis. For Brenner, then, the demographic crisis of the fourteenth century was a result of feudal class relations. Furthermore, whereas Postan saw the scarcity of peasants after the demographic crisis as leading to the overthrow of serfdom, Brenner sees the winning of peasant freedom as a result of class power and the balance of class forces. The different outcomes in different parts of Europe *vis-à-vis* the crisis of the fourteenth and fifteenth centuries, were, Brenner argues, the result of different balances of class forces. In this context he sees levels of solidarity amongst the peasantry, their self-consciousness and organisation and their general political resources – i.e. their relations with non-agricultural classes (especially urban allies) and the state – as significant. He sees the divergent development of Eastern and Western Europe as a product of differing levels of peasant solidarity and strength, especially at village level.

His discussion of Eastern and Western Germany is instructive. By the late middle ages Western Germany was undergoing protracted struggle on a village-by-village basis. Peasants succeeded in securing a degree of economic self-regulation and political self-government through, for example, village courts. This gave them a powerful line of defence against lords. Peasant organisation and resistance in Western Germany was bound up with the common fields system and the quasi-communal character of the peasant economy (e.g. rights of common). This produced a degree of internal cohesion amongst the peasantry, enabling them to fix their own rents and secure rights of inheritance, as well as elect their own mayor and choose their own village priest. Importantly, all of this meant that the peasantry in Western Germany were able to resist feudal reaction in the fourteenth century.

In Eastern Germany, however, economic cooperation amongst the peasantry and self-government of peasant villages developed only to a small extent. The communal aspects of village life were underdeveloped, there being no common lands, and the common fields system was less developed. Basically farming was more individualistic. Villages were also smaller. With a single lord, rather than several, village peasants had less room to manoeuvre and bargain.

Brenner applies this model to Europe in general. Throughout most of Western Europe peasants' solidarity made possible stubborn resistance on a village-by-village basis, enabling them to limit the claims of the aristocracy and bring about the dissolution of serfdom. In Eastern Europe the peasantry lacked cooperation and resistance on a village basis. They succumbed to seigniorial reaction and the reimposition of serfdom.

The question that remains, however, is why England developed agrarian capitalism based on free wage labour and large units of production in the sixteenth and seventeenth centuries when other Western European societies did not. Contrasting England and France, Brenner's explanation rests on the specificity of class conflicts and struggles. In England landowners defeated peasant class resistance, undermining peasant proprietorship. In France landowners were unable to undermine peasant property rights and create large capitalist farms.

Following the demographic collapse of the fourteenth and fifteenth centuries, English landlords were able to consolidate their holdings. By the sixteenth century the English peasantry were in open revolt, with major agrarian risings threatening the entire social order. If successful this could have clipped the wings of rural capitalism. But the peasantry did not secure freehold control and by the end of the seventeenth century English landlords controlled between 70 and 75 per cent of cultivable land. The consequences were momentous for the development of agrarian capitalism.

In his 1976 study Brenner focused on the role of the state in this process. He sees the French absolutist state as developing relatively independently of landowners. Policies of protecting rural communities from excessive exploitation by landlords had the effect of maintaining the existence of the peasant class and retarding rural social differentiation. Surplus extraction from the peasantry was used for non-productive purposes, holding back capital accumulation on the part of the peasantry.

Brenner saw the English state as much more closely associated with the landlord interest of economic expansion. Unprepared to protect the new free peasantry, the state supported landlords through enclosure and consolidation of holdings. This undermined peasant property and established absolute private property rights. A wage-labour force and agrarian capitalism emerged.

In his 1982 study,[18] however, Brenner's 'political' focus was on the importance of 'political accumulation'. This is defined as 'the build up of larger more effective military organisation and/or the construction of surplus extraction machinery'. In England this process was much stronger than in France, producing a much stronger landowner class. Their retention of feudal rights and powers after the decline of serfdom enabled them to institute consolidation of land freehold tenure. In France, where such processes of 'political accumulation' did not develop, the tenurial security of the peasantry remained more or less in one piece.

SOME FEMINIST QUESTIONS

The explanations of the transition that I have outlined have been much debated and criticised. I have touched on some of that debate and critique myself. I have not, however, set out to provide a systematic exposition of that material here; it can be easily followed up in the literature. What I am concerned about is this: nowhere within the debate on the transition have *feminist* questions been posed. Consequently, a systematic account of patriarchy is missing from our understanding of the shift from feudalism to capitalism.

The kinds of questions we would need to consider if we are to develop such an account would include the following. Did the rise and fall of population levels in medieval Europe have any impact upon patriarchal relations? What was the impact of long-distance trade upon patriarchal relations (cross-culturally and historically, long-distance trade has usually been a male preserve). What were the similarities and differences in gender relations between town and countryside? How did or do gender relations differ between 'core' and 'peripheral' nation states and of what significance is this? How did the overthrow of serfdom affect gender relations? How did the reimposition of serfdom in Eastern Europe affect gender relations? How did different forms of feudal rent affect relations between the sexes? To what extent did social differentiation amongst the peasantry affect the degree and intensity of patriarchy amongst different socio-economic categories? How did patriarchal relations vary within and between the peasantry, the merchant class, small capitalist farmers, the gentry and the aristocracy? Were class conflict and class solidarity articulated and mobilised through forms of patriarchal ideology such as that of the free*man*? And what of the role of the state? How did it advance and further patriarchal interests? How did the patriarchal nature of the state in feudal society change over time? In England, for example, were there any significant differences with respect to patriarchy between the Norman and Tudor states? What broad similarities and differences with respect to patriarchal relations were there between feudal politics in different countries? What broad similarities and differences might there have been between feudal polities in different countries? What broad similarities and differences might there be between feudal and capitalist states *vis-à-vis* patriarchal relations? Have the similarities and differences between different capitalist states today been shaped by different forms of patriarchal relations in feudal societies?

Of course much existing work by historians – feminists or otherwise – will have a bearing upon such questions. But for a full understanding we need more detailed research. We also need to piece such research together so as to draw out broad patterns, trends and implications. Historians, though, have often been resistant to advancing large-scale theoretically informed epochal analysis. That approach has usually been the terrain of sociologists. Though inevitably and necessarily drawing upon the detailed work of historians, when comparing different societies cross-culturally and historically, sociologists tend to concentrate on the general and constitutive features of societies, drawing broad comparisons, painting broad brush-strokes. This is the type of approach I have adopted in this study.

Although I have raised here a number of questions which need to be at least considered if we are to develop a full understanding of patriarchy in the transition to capitalism, I do not intend to address those questions directly myself (even though my study has a bearing upon them). My focus as a sociologist will be upon property. I have already outlined the significance of property for an analysis of social divisions, in particular those of patriarchy and class. There are sufficient data within the existing literature to enable us to work up an analysis of patriarchal relations with respect to different historical forms of property in England.

Concepts such as property do not have universal applicability: what is meant by property will vary both *between* societies and *within* any particular society over time. As Marx states:

> In each historical epoch, property has developed differently and under a set of entirely different social relations. Thus to define bourgeois property is nothing else than to give an exposition of all the social relations of bourgeois production. To try and give a definition of property as of an independent relation, a category apart, an abstract and eternal idea, can be nothing but an illusion of metaphysics or jurisprudence.[19]

And as Derek Sayer writes:

> In previous forms of society, neither individuals as owners nor their property had their modern exclusivity or simplicity. Property did not even appear as a simple relation of persons and things. Who owned what, or even what it meant to be an owner, were by no means clear cut; the very terms at issue are anachronistic.[20]

Max Bloch's observations of medieval Europe are instructive: he points out that the word 'ownership' in relation to landed property was not really applicable. This was because numerous people, fathers, sons, a hierarchy of lords and the village community could all lay claim to a piece of land.[21]

In feudal society the system of property rights was a divided one. The king was the nominal 'owner' of all of the land. In return for military service or money paid to the king, feudal lords were also considered to be property owners – suzerains in fact – with jurisdiction over serfs and tenants. However, the situation was further complicated by a fundamental feature of feudal society – the direct producer, the peasant, was '... in possession of his [sic] own means of production, the necessary material labour conditions required for the realisation of his labour and the production of his means [sic] of subsistence'.[22] In capitalist society the situation is much more clear cut. It is a relationship of exclusive, individual possession. It is only in capitalist society that property appears as a simple relation of possession between individuals and objects. According to legal historians this new conception of ownership could be detected in seventeenth century England. S. F. C. Milson considers that the powers of owners had undergone a detectable change. An owner could now assert his (sic) proprietorial claims over a wider range of persons. The range of persons an owner could hold liable to return the value of his property was extended.[23] According to Sir William Holdsworth, in the seventeenth century 'the common law had come to recognise that ownership was an absolute right as against all the world, and not merely the better right of a plaintiff as against the defendant in possession'.[24] Milson and Holdsworth both share the view that the nature of ownership was changing in the seventeenth century. Gerald Aylmer's study of property in seventeenth-century English law dictionaries confirms this.[25] The political theorist C. B. Macpherson has also argued that 'the concept of property ... changed in discernible ways with the rise of modern capitalism'.[26] In line with others, he sees the capitalist form of property as being:

> identical with private property – an individual (or corporate) right to exclude others from the use, or benefit of something [and] ... a right in or to material things rather than a right to a revenue.[27]

We can see then that the nature of property varies historically. But *what* actually counts as property? In 'The German Ideology' Marx discusses property in terms of the 'material, instruments and products of labour'.[28] This definition is very broad indeed. Material, instruments and products of labour have varied over time and geographically. The sea, boats or fish, for example, would not have been considered property by stone-age peoples. Nor would radium, nuclear reactors or nuclear bombs. Crucially there is nothing intrinsic about the sea, radium, boats, nuclear reactors, fish or nuclear bombs which makes them property. They only become property within a specific social and historical context. Property is not a 'thing', it is a Social Relation.

Marx's discussion of ownership in 'The German Ideology' as *'relations of individuals to one another with reference to* the material, instruments and products of labour' (my emphasis) captures this well.[29] We can think of such relations as involving persons with *rights* in, or to, the materials, instruments and products of labour (the 'ownables'), and *duties* flowing from such rights.[30] The ownables, persons, rights and duties I shall be focusing on in this study will include land, chattels, women, men, families, social classes, inheritance, revenue, use, alienation, protection, taxation and liabilities. 'Persons', rights and duties in relation to property may be defined de facto, in a moral or practical way, or de jure, in legal terms. Historically speaking, relationships have more often than not been defined de jure *after* their prior de facto definition. Marx illustrates this point well:

> [with Wagner] there is, first, the law, and then *commerce*, and then a *legal order* develops out of it. In the analysis of the circulation of commodities (in *Capital*) I have demonstrated that in a developed trade the exchangers tacitly recognise each other as equal persons and owners of the goods to be exchanged respectively by them; they *do* this while they offer the goods to one another and agree to trade with one another. The *practical* relation, arising through and in exchange itself, only later attains a *legal form* in contracts etc.[31]

Taking the patriarchy–class relationship as central, in the following chapters I shall consider property – ownables, persons, rights and duties, de jure[32] and de facto – in the context of Anglo-Saxon,[33] feudal and capitalist society in England.

Chapter 4

Property and patriarchy

This chapter comprises an analysis of patriarchy and rights in and to property. First of all I shall consider material which relates to the Anglo-Saxon situation. I will then move on to analysis of the feudal period. Finally I shall look at the development of the form of property characteristic of capitalism.

PROPERTY AND PATRIARCHY BEFORE THE NORMAN CONQUEST

Some historians consider that the Anglo-Saxon period brought a significant improvement in property rights for women. McNamara and Wemple, for example, note that 'as the smaller family group began to replace the tribe as the basic social unit, the incapacity of women to inherit property began to disappear'.[1] More recently, Christine Fell has discussed the extensive landholdings of upper-class women,[2] and queens as owners and givers of estates.[3]

In both theoretical and empirical terms this view is disputable. As Viana Muller points out, 'It would be just as logical for these historians to praise the development of the state for liberating men, who could as a result own private property and become wealthy, whereas in tribal society they couldn't really own anything as an individual'.[4]

Empirically too, whilst women were by no means excluded from ownership of property, evidence relating to both inheritance and acquisition shows men still at an advantage over women. Bookland, being property which was acquired rather than inherited, was not governed by rules of kinship. Early records indicate that gifts of bookland were first made to religious orders in an attempt to provide the Christian church with a permanent landed endowment.[5] Mark Meyer notes that with the king's increasing need for military strength, and the expanding law to be administered, during the tenth and eleventh centuries thegns were also increasingly rewarded with bookland.[6] Patrick Wormald, though, traces the appearance of bookland for secular aristocrats from the late *eighth* century and, as we shall see, suggests that this may be related to shifts in inheritance patterns. Bookland could be alienated. Through choice rather than through the custom of the kin it could become a hereditary tenure.[7]

Though not expressed legally, the relationship between a grantee of bookland and those who held land under him could come to resemble those of a feudal lord and tenant.[8] Effectively, bookland could become a grant of lordship and revenues, and sometimes jurisdiction and profits. Lords of bookland sometimes created out of it smaller holdings of the same type, and it is apparent that many people living on such land owed dues and services to these lords.[9] It is important to note that bookland did not mark the *beginning* of lordship: T. M. Charles Edwards points to the existence of lordship in the seventh century, and Dorothy Whitelock suggests the social relation of lordship may have existed long before that. Rather, bookland marked a consolidation of the power of the Anglo-Saxon nobility.[10]

According to Mark Meyer, although the low survival rate of Anglo-Saxon charters makes an estimate of the amount of bookland held by women difficult, the evidence that does exist suggests that only a small percentage of either secular or ecclesiastic women were, as individuals, grantees of bookland.[11] Such grants as were made to women would be either for the purposes of endowing a religious community, or else for the furtherance of royal interest in some other way. King Edward (934–946), for example, issued eight bookland charters to ecclesiastic women, and in 985 Aethelred II issued a charter to Wulfrun, a woman from a prominent Staffordshire family. Domesday too states that a particular thegn might be a client of a queen, abbess, or laywoman. (Eadgifu the Fair possessed extensive manors in Cambridgeshire and loaned portions of her estates to men in return for their taking on services that she owed to the king.)

However, Meyer argues that both social and marital status limited not only the extent to which women were granted bookland in their own right, but also their ability, where it was held jointly with a husband, to exploit the potential power of book-

land. Where women individually were granted bookland, it was
either because of their association with the royal household or
because they were members of the powerful provincial aristocracy.[12] He says that women received bookland jointly with their
husbands because of their relationship to a loyal thegn of the
king and because of their maternal role within the family. In this
context he points out that a husband was very much the senior
partner, though a woman was recognised as being capable of
managing an estate in her husband's absence. However, a wife
was usually mentioned in a passive connection in the charters.
Where estates were gifted to religious communities, for example,
wives usually appear as consenting parties, complying with the
wishes of their husbands.[13]

As far as inherited property is concerned, the Venerable Bede
implies that inheritance was divided between sons, with the eldest
probably receiving the paternal home.[14] According to the laws of
Ine 'if a husband and wife have a child and rear it; she is to be
given six shillings for its maintenance, a cow in summer, an ox
in winter; the kinsmen are to take charge of the paternal home,
until the child is grown up'.[15] Whilst it seems to have been customary for sons to share their father's land, the exact nature of
the division varied. Primogeniture, at least according to some
historians, was not yet established.[16]

Legal authorities such as Pollock and Maitland also say that
primogeniture was not yet properly established, even at the end
of the Anglo-Saxon period. But they do note events significant
in its development. They suggest that impartible succession, in
which land was inherited by the youngest or eldest son, existed
amongst those who became the *villani* and *servi* of Domesday
Book. Domesday Book certainly records that several thegns
sometimes held land 'in parage', i.e. as co-heirs holding an undiv-
ided inheritance, in which case only one of them – usually the
eldest, from whom the younger heirs held 'in parage' – was
responsible for military duty.[17]. Anglo-Saxonist Patrick Wormald
suggests that by the eighth century there may have been an
increasing presumption that an eldest son would have major rights
in inheritance. He points out that records of the Kentish custom
of Gavelkind, in which the rule was partibility between sons, with
the youngest receiving the family home, would imply that rules
for the rest of England were different. Significantly, recognition
of this custom coincides with the appearance of bookland for

secular aristocrats in the eighth century. Wormald suggests that the increasing practice of giving the eldest son major rights in inheritance would likely prompt noblemen to acquire bookland as a way of providing for younger sons and daughters.[18]

Whichever interpretation of the evidence as regards primogeniture is accepted, there does seem to have been a preferential treatment of male heirs. Unsurprisingly, the Domesday Book reveals that very few women were tenant landholders in their own right. But historical evidence also shows that kinship remained an important consideration in the transmission of property. Thus, whilst bookland was a way of catering for the needs of daughters, in cases where there were no male heirs women of the same degree of kinship might inherit in their stead.[19] However, although women did have access to the descent group's property, usually they benefited only as *dependants* of male heads of nuclear families.

PROPERTY AND PATRIARCHY IN FEUDAL ENGLAND

By the thirteenth century, inherited and acquired property were no longer potentially subject to different rules of succession.[20] By the end of that century, as far as free tenures were concerned, primogeniture had become the law of England. Lawyers applied the rule of primogeniture unless special proof of a custom of partibility was given.[21] Glanville, during the twelfth century, states 'if he was a knight ... the eldest succeeds to his father in everything'.[22] According to Bracton, writing in the thirteenth century, 'in the matter of succession the male sex must always be preferred to the female'[23] and 'Proprietary right ... lies with the older'.[24] By the early sixteenth century the principle of primogeniture seems to have spread downwards to the gentry,[25] and by the eighteenth century to members of the yeomanry[26].

The establishment of primogeniture needs initially to be understood in terms of the political exigencies of the patron–client relation which became the basic organising principle of feudal England. During the Anglo-Saxon period, as tenure of land became increasingly tied to military service, it is likely that the king would be unwilling to accept an arrangement amongst thegns which fractionalised military duty. The holding of land 'in parage' from an elder brother would also have facilitated the collection of relief, aides and taxes.[27] Following the Norman Conquest,

primogeniture was the rule where military tenants-in-chief owed
personal service in the king's army for land and rights of
jurisdiction.

Women did not enter into the patron–client relationship where
it involved military service because of the biological differences
between women and men. I am *not* however arguing, as radical
feminists often do when discussing the origins of women's
oppression, that the cause of women's subordination in this context was biological.[28] Rather, I am arguing, on the basis of historical evidence, that biological differences between women and men
became socially significant in England with the entrenchment
of class relations. Military feudalism expressed a class relation,
exercised through the patron–client principle, and contributed to
the detriment of women.

Patron–client relations were integral to state formation. Pollock
and Maitland argue that the near-absolute and uncompromising
form of primogeniture which emerged in England was not characteristic of feudalism in general, but of a highly centralised version
of feudalism in which, theoretically at least, the king had little to
fear from even his mightiest vassals.[29] Although subinfeudation
may have led lesser tenants to conceive of themselves as fighting
for their mesne lords, all military service was performed for the
king.[30] The distribution of land was also of central importance
for the imposition of taxes.[31] Thus primogeniture was also crucial
to determining the taxable capacity of subjects of the English
state.

The permanent commutation of personal service into money
had by the thirteenth century replaced the former military relevance of primogeniture. However, the interests of wealthy landowners ensured the preservation of the principle.[32] Primogeniture
was profoundly political. Both before and after the Norman Conquest, it facilitated the preservation and accumulation of property,
sustaining and reproducing relations of class power.

John Aubrey pointed out that entails (a legal device to restrict
the transmission of estates to a specified line of heirs) were a
good prop for monarchy.[33] In the sixteenth century Lipset recognised that primogeniture preserved the class hierarchy. The stability of the state depended on the existence of well-rooted and
well-endowed families in positions of authority.[34] He warned that
without primogeniture 'you shall in the process of years confound
the nobles and the commons together after such manner that

there shall be no difference betwixt the one and the other'.[35] Indeed, in the nineteenth century it was stated that primogeniture 'had a peculiar value ... in preserving the independence of the aristocratic branch of the constitution'. The absence of primogeniture and settlement 'would leave many peerages without an estate to support their honours'.[36]

Primogeniture would no doubt have been practised by the magnates at the core of the country gentry during the English revolution of the seventeenth century, which was to undermine the political power of the Crown and aristocracy. Christopher Hill points out that strict settlement – designed to protect and preserve the principle of primogeniture, particularly after the abolition of feudal tenures – was crucial for the development of agrarian capitalism. It 'led on to the great consolidation of landed property which made the Whig oligarchy of the eighteenth century ... it also contributed to the relative depression of the lesser gentry'.[37]

When in the nineteenth century it was proposed that the law on intestacy in connection with real estate be made the same as for personal property, where equal division occurred, such proposals were always violently and successfully resisted by the landed interest. Any interference with primogeniture would, it was felt, by leading to the division of estates 'destroy that fair and reasonable influence which the property and aristocracy of the country was allowed to possess'. According to Palmerston, such changes would be incompatible with the existence of the landed gentry and 'tended to republicanism'.[38]

> If Montesquieu approved entails and primogeniture as means to preserve noble families, themselves essential to true monarchies, he also expressed the republican tradition, partly derived from Harrington, that such devices were inimical to republican regimes which required more or less egalitarian partible inheritance.[39]

Although it has been argued that the primary intention of primogeniture was the establishment and maintenance of class privilege, Joan Thirsk notes that amongst the nobility primogeniture 'seems to have been deemed by common consent the most acceptable practice for *family reasons* [my emphasis] ... it reduced strife among brothers when the eldest automatically took the leading positions; it maintained the status of the family'.[40] In this context she cites Lipset from the sixteenth century: 'If the lands in every great family were distributed equally betwixt the brethren in a small process of years the head families would decay and little by little vanish away',[41] as well as Powell: 'Partition in a populous country already furnished with inhabitants is the very decay of the great families, and ... the cause of strife and debate.'[42] Similarly, entails helped to prevent families with hereditary roles in government becoming impoverished due to the extravagance of an heir.[43]

Thirsk points out that primogeniture was not popular with the peasantry, and that during the Interregnum it was subject to adverse comment by pamphleteers as 'the most unreasonable descent'.[44] Primogeniture amongst the peasantry seems to have been related to the degree of manorialisation. It probably developed under strong seigniorial pressure and was roughly associated with large demesnes and heavy labour services. In areas of weak manorialisation the practice of partible inheritance still existed during the sixteenth century.[45] Thirsk also states that:

> a clear distinction can be observed between the weakly man-
> orialized districts of England and Wales where family cohesion
> was aided by the practice of partible inheritance, which
> involved much cooperation within the family, in the working
> of jointly owned land, and the highly manorialized areas, where
> the family observed primogeniture, and farming co-operation
> was not a family, but a village concern.[46]

Faith similarly argues that 'there obviously is a connection between strong lordship and weak kinship and vice versa'.[47] However, she also says that it is misleading to draw a rigid distinction between the two systems. She points out that on partible holdings elder sons might become the sole heirs by buying out their younger brothers' shares. Meanwhile, in areas of primogeniture, younger children and other relatives could be provided for, either by settling land on them before death, or, very often, by use of the will.[48] Indeed Faith says that

> However much peasant inheritance customs varied by the thir-
> teenth century, they shared one basic principle. They placed
> great importance on the concept of keeping the name on the
> land ... the emphasis on family landholding is as strong in
> areas of partibility as elsewhere.[49]

To clarify further why the bulk of property in feudal England was held by men, it is worth considering Goody's discussion of bilateral inheritance and diverging devolution. Diverging devolution, common in the centralised state societies of Eurasia, is associated with intensive plough agriculture and complex systems of stratification. Under systems of diverging devolution, property is distributed to children of both sexes, females can receive property from males and males can receive property from females, as opposed to homogeneous devolution in which property is transmitted from males to males or from females to females. In England, as with the main Eurasian societies, a close female was entitled to inherit before a more distant male, even where both were members of the same descent group.[50]

Women also had access to property through the medium of dowry and dower. Dower was a settlement on the bride by her husband's descent group. It embodied a recognition that the husband's estate should bear responsibility for the support of the bride and her children.[51] During the Anglo-Saxon period the 'morning gift' was given by the husband to his wife the morning after the consummation of marriage, presumably once virginity had been ascertained.[52] Paid to the woman herself, the morning gift was a way of giving a married woman some financial security.[53] If she left her husband, her morning gift was distributed amongst her kindred – probably because they would have to repay the brideprice[54] (a marriage transaction which I shall discuss later). After the Norman Conquest the morning gift died out in favour of the widow's dower (though of course the widow's portion was fairly institutionalised in Anglo-Saxon society too). Dowry, meanwhile, was a method of ensuring that daughters inherited some of their own descent group's property. It was allocated when they married.

Under systems of diverging devolution, then, property can potentially be diffused, through marriage, outside the descent group.[55] It is therefore unsurprising that daughters only inherited landed property as residual heirs, since any property they may have inherited might have been passed on to their children who were members of the husband's descent group, thus transferring it out of their own. If inheritance practices had been primarily patriarchal in *intent*, the question arises why men should have allowed women to inherit anything at all. But this should not prevent us perceiving male advantage associated with this system.

It clearly made good *class* and *family* sense; but it did so by privileging the position of males. As Gerder Lerner points out, 'giving sons and daughters inheritance rights in order to preserve the family property does not mean that they have *equal* rights'.[56] This bias, I would suggest, contributed to subsequent gender inequalities in access to material resources, furnishing part of the basis for the development of gendered class divisions.

From the twelfth to the late fourteenth century it appears that sons *and daughters* inherited *moveable* property on an equal basis. According to one common custom during the thirteenth century, that part of a dead man's property which he left to his children was divided between sons and daughters equally.[57] Clearly, moveable property did not have the same significance as landed property for the maintenance and furtherance of class privilege. It could be argued, then, that men had no reason to exclude women from the inheritance of moveable property in order to protect their privilege as *men*. However, it might also be argued that if inheritance strategies were *primarily* concerned with the maintenance of *male* privilege, then we might expect women to have been excluded from gaining any kind of property.

Furthermore, although possession of *landed* property was for the most part vested in men, the reversionary rights of lords, and in particular the king, ultimately limited the scope of *all* heirs – women *and* men. Though property might be alienated, and an active land market existed,[58] neither common law (king's law) nor equity recognised absolute titles. In the seventeenth century the uncertainty of legal title was such that Lord Chief Justice Hale, after a purchase of land, is reported to have said that he would be happy to pay the equivalent of another year's purchase price in order to be sure of the title![59] However, now in place was a structure which, with the emergence of more individualised concepts of property, could provide a basis for a more explicit articulation of gender inequality.

PROPERTY RELATIONS ARISING THROUGH MARRIAGE

According to Christine Fell, in Anglo-Saxon England 'the laws recognise an element of financial independence and responsibility in the wife's status'.[60] Earlier sources also suggest that Anglo-Saxon widows had control over their dower property.[61] Fell believes that women had personal control over their morning gifts.[62] She also quotes Whitred: 'If a man sacrifices to devils without his wife's knowledge he is liable to pay all his goods; if they both sacrifice to devils they are liable to pay all their goods.' This, she says, indicates that a wife's goods were not under masculine control or that their goods were held in common.[63] She also cites Wulfric's will as 'one of the clearest indications that women – wives and daughters – inherited and held property independently and separately from husband and father'.[64]

However, it has already been indicated that women's control over property was ultimately constrained by the marital relationship. According to Mark Meyer a widow could not alienate dower property outside the family without the sanction of her husband.[65] Patrick Wormald says that although 'there are a quite significant number of charters and wills in which Anglo-Saxon women dispose of property', he has found 'no case where they can be proven to do so against the will of a living husband'.[66]

The *Lawes Resolutions of Women's Rights*, compiled during the Tudor period and published in 1632, summed up the position of married women for much of the medieval and early modern period: 'That which the husband hath is his own. That which the wife hath is the husband's.'[67] With the exception of the Queen of England, who from the fourteenth century had independent property rights,[68] men became guardians of their wives' estates.

It is not clear whether wives could actually own moveable goods before the thirteenth century. Before 1200, moveable succession was the province of the church. Ecclesiastical law recognised a married woman's testimonary capacity. However, if a woman made a will it is likely that it would prove valid only if her husband did not dispute it. During the thirteenth century, with the exception of paraphernalia, i.e. dress and personal ornaments – which would go to the wife if they had not been alienated by her husband – the common law gave husbands absolute possession of their wives' moveable goods. As a result a husband could not give anything to his wife during marriage.[69]

Although there were legal devices to prevent a husband from alienating his wife's *landed property* absolutely,[70] husbands were nevertheless entitled to rents and profits. Husbands also gained possession of dowry through marriage. If the gift had been made expressly to the wife, husband and children, a husband's interest lasted until his death, even if he survived both his wife and the

children of the marriage. Unless dowry was assigned as part of a
widow's dower, a woman had no control over it when her husband
died. It descended to the heir of the marriage or, if there were
no children, to the woman's natal kin.[71]

Given that a married woman had no proprietary capacity, she
could not sue or be sued at common law in her own name,
nor could she sue her own husband.[72] Nor could she make
contracts for her own benefit.[73] Restrictions of this sort came
under what was known as the law of coverture. There were a few
exceptions, as where corporation byelaws allowed married women
to trade on their own account, with certain proprietary and legal
rights independent of their husbands. However, in the seventeenth century the common law increasingly took precedence,
depriving married woman of such proprietary rights as they had
previously had.

To understand the law of coverture we need to consider how
it slotted into the historical specificity of property relations. We
have already seen that the male bias in property relations
extended beyond the marital relationship in Anglo-Saxon society.
In later chapters we shall also see that through the processes of
state formation, well under way in Anglo-Saxon society, the
nuclear family became much more clearly separated from wider
kin groups, groups which also appear to have been rather more
male-centred than female. One of the effects of state formation
was to exacerbate any pre-existing tendency towards gender bias:
women became much more obviously dependent upon individual
men, fathers and husbands, for material support. We have already
seen too that neither common law nor equity recognised absolute
titles. Feudal titles referred to revenue rights, not exclusive ownership. Husbands were *guardians* of their wives' estates. They were
entitled to rents and profit, but not absolute title. This is not
meant to imply that women could not be disadvantaged by the
set-up. At the very least it could bolster male status. But in
recognising women's disadvantage we must avoid imposing concepts of inequality which are bound up with specifically *capitalist*
property forms.

We should also bear in mind how the allocation and control of
dowry made 'sense' within the system of social ranking at the
time. Dowry can be seen as a way of restricting the likelihood of
daughters marrying too far 'down' or 'out'. Jack Goody points out
that dowry is both a product and an instrument of stratification. In

enabling a man to ensure the maintenance of his daughters,[74] it also maintains or even promotes the status of the family. But I would suggest, too, that it was another mechanism which served to bolster male privilege, through the prestige attaching to the portion given. Dowry could either descend to the heir of the marriage[75] or could be used to buy land. This combined interests of both class and kinship. It did so in a manner not incompatible – conducive even – to the prestige of men.

Before the mid-thirteenth century, dowry could take the form of land.[76] Later, as Stone indicates, dowry usually took the form of a cash sum,[77] presumably because of the increasing function of landed property as an instrument of stratification. Amongst the peasantry, dowry probably took the form of moveables.[78] Stone points out that amongst the sixteenth-century aristocracy, differences in rank were reflected in differences of up to 40 per cent in the size of dowries. In the latter part of the century, however, this difference shrank. He thinks that the size of portions offered by the peerage was being forced up due to competition from the squirearchy, and continued to be forced up throughout the seventeenth century. In the seventeenth century the peerage was spending a much higher proportion of its income in marrying off daughters than had been the case in the sixteenth century.[79] Historians also point out that marriage was a significant factor in the rise of the great estates during the eighteenth century. Portions were normally larger in relation to settlements on widows than in the seventeenth century. It has been suggested that one of the reasons for this was that, in comparison to most of the sixteenth century and early seventeenth century, in the early eighteenth century the material interests which were looked for in marriage were more exclusively to do with wealth. Political power was becoming more dependent on landed wealth, whereas in the sixteenth and early seventeenth century royal favour had counted for more. Marriage to a woman who had a large dowry usually resulted in the acquisition of land – portions could be spent on buying land – which descended to the eldest son and remained within the family. If, on the other hand, a man married an heiress, the land that came with her might not accrue to him, as it might be settled away from his eldest son after his own and his wife's death.[80] Given that dowry was intended to protect the interests of women but could also bolster male privilege, a point of speculation is to what extent was the size of dowry associated with an intensification of patriarchal relations?

Portions given to the bride by the husband are also bound up with social stratification. Given the increasing importance of landed property as a determinant of class position, it is not surprising that the morning gift, which could be distributed amongst a woman's paternal kin, died out after the Norman Conquest in favour of the widow's dower. Restrictions could be placed on the widow's rights of disposal. In the Anglo-Saxon period, for example, widows might be requested to keep bookland allocated to them in the male line.[81]

The actual size of the widow's dower both during the Anglo-Saxon period and following the Norman Conquest seems to have varied. Amongst the upper classes it could be either half or one-third of a husband's estate.[82] By the thirteenth century, where land was held by military tenure, one-third of the husband's lands was the maximum dower.[83] Presumably, the reduction from half was a measure to lessen the consequences if land fell into the hands of a stranger or enemy following the remarriage of a widow. It also became possible to specify the amount of dower at the church door,[84] a pointer to the importance of publicly regulated rights. Pollock and Maitland suggest that, given the frequency with which specific lands are mentioned as dower, many widows from the upper ranks of society may have had to be content with less than their thirds.[85] Whilst class considerations may have been important in this context, the impact on the material position of women would have tended to be deleterious. Lower down the social hierarchy widows appear to have fared better.

On customary tenures widows' rights were usually greater than those at common law. Widows of customary tenants might be entitled to half or two-thirds of the deceased husband's estate.[86] Although the effect could ultimately have been detrimental to the heir, common tenancy could be arranged. Hilton also suggests that the practice of issuing leases for several lifetimes – thereby giving wives a life interest after the death of a husband – gave extra security to widows.[87] Littleton also indicates that wives of burgesses might have greater rights: 'by the custom in some town or borough she shall have the whole'.[88] However, the decline of customary tenures, though far from complete by the beginning of the eighteenth century, put many widows in a precarious position.[89] This process cannot be divorced from changes in the law which were associated with the development of capitalism.

CAPITALISM, PROPERTY AND PATRIARCHY

So far I have argued that the patriarchal structuring of property relations was inherent in pre-capitalist property forms in England. These in turn were embedded in a matrix of historically specific class structures and kinship relations. I want now to consider the implications of this bias in the transition from feudalism to capitalism in England. I will suggest that the capitalist concept of individual property, accentuating this bias, contributed greatly to the fractionalisation of class relations along gender lines.

Feudal titles were not the same as modern private ownership of estates. Feudal property rights usually meant rights to a revenue in the form of services, produce or money.[90] Property relations did not usually involve rights to *things*. Property rights were usually limited to certain uses of land. Different people could have different rights in the same piece of land which was not fully disposable either by sale or bequest.[91] A quote from Marc Bloch amplifies this:

> The word ownership as applied to landed property, would have been almost meaningless ... The tenant who, from father to son, as a rule ploughs the land, and gathers in the crops; his immediate lord, to whom he pays dues and who, in certain circumstances, can resume possession of the land; the lord of the lord, and so on, right up the feudal scale – how many persons are there who can say, each with as much justification as the other, 'That is my field!' Even this is an understatement. For the ramifications extended horizontally as well as vertically and account should be taken of the village community, which normally recovered the use of the whole of its agricultural land as soon as it was cleared of crops; of the tenant's family, without whose consent the property could not be alienated; and of the families of the successive lords.[92]

Alan Macfarlane, however, in *The Origins of English Individualism*, has argued that from the thirteenth century onwards both freehold land and customary tenures belonged to an individual, not to a family group. He contends that 'There were no inalienable birth rights, either of the eldest child or any other';[93] that de facto, under customary law, 'both villeins and freemen could and did pass on land to their heirs or other people, either by gift or sale'.[94] Indeed, Macfarlane argues that 'England was as "capitalist" in 1250 as it was in 1550 or 1750... land was treated as a commodity and full private ownership was established'.[95]

Technically, i.e. in relation to the absence of a jural link between the family and the land, Macfarlane may be correct. However, that does *not* make medieval England a capitalist society. Macfarlane acknowledges himself that he has not found the origins of English individualism, despite the title of his book.[96] He suspects, however, that the origins lie in the 'Germanic system as described by Tacitus of absolute individual property'.[97] If he had followed through his suspicion, he would have discovered that alienability and heritability emerged in Anglo-Saxon England concurrently with the development of an increasingly stratified *class* society, not a capitalist society. If Macfarlane had fully grasped the *transitional* nature of the Germanic or feudal form of 'communal' property, his conflation of individualism and capitalism could have been avoided. In the *Grundrisse* Marx notes that the 'individual is ... only a possessor. What persists is only communal property and only *private possession*'.[98] Similarly, Macfarlane may be technically correct that children had no inalienable birth rights; however, it has been demonstrated that, de facto, kinship remained an important consideration in the transmission of property.

Moreover, even in the fifteenth century the enormous incomes of the great landed aristocrats were still based on rent.[99] As Rodney Hilton argues, following Marx, 'The essence of the feudal mode of production... is the exploitative relationship between landowners and subordinated peasants, in which surplus beyond subsistence of the latter, whether in direct labour or in rent in kind or in money, is transferred under coercive sanction to the former.'[100]

However, with the development of capitalism in England, feudal property was transformed into modern individualistic ownership. Property became a right in or to material *things*, i.e. objects or commodities. Property becomes an absolute right, and this sort of property is exactly the sort required to facilitate the development of a capitalist market economy.[101] Property as the right of legal individuals involves the right to exclude others.[102]

We can quite clearly see this shift occurring. By the 1640s, for the more prosperous yeomen, merchants, gentry and peers, instead of being primarily a source of service, loyalty or followers, land was becoming more a profit-yielding investment, i.e. capital.[103] The sale of appropriated church land by Henry VIII to the gentry contributed to the development of a class of capitalist farmers; and by the early seventeenth century Cowell writes:

> Propertie signifieth the highest right that a man hath or can have to any thing which is in no way depending upon any other mans courtesie. And this none in our kingdom can be said to have in any lands, or tenements, but onely the king in the right of his Crowne. Because all the lands through the realm, are in the nature of fee, and dow hould either mediately or immediately of the Crowne ... This work is in our common law, used for that right in lands and tenements, that common persons have because it imparteth as much as *utile dominium* though not *directum*.[104]

In 1652, however, Zouche defined property as 'Common rights to things, is that which is agreeable to the law of Nations, as Property which is the right of enjoying and disposing of a thing at pleasure, and is gained by Industry'.[105] Cromwell's legal adviser, Sheppard, produced something like an official law dictionary, in which it was stated 'Property is the right that a man hath to anything which in no way dependeth upon another man's courtesie: And he that hath this is called a Proprietary'.[106] In a republican work in 1670 there is the following:

> So that it seems it is called the king's highway, because of the privilege that the king hath in it for his people to pass and repass through it, and not in respect of any property he hath in the soil itself; yet divers, as of Mannors do claim the soil.[107]

IMPLICATIONS FOR GENDER RELATIONS

The development of individualised property rights associated with the transition from feudalism to capitalism had a formative effect on subsequent gender relations. Consider again the long historical construction of masculinised – patriarchal – property relations. Then consider the implications of a transition to the individualistic and absolute form of property characteristic of capitalism.

It has been argued that primogeniture, for example, was first and foremost a strategy designed to maintain and further relations of class power. It also structured relations hierarchically between men and, crucially, between the sexes. It did so across the social spectrum. Although there were debates and campaigns against primogeniture during the sixteenth, seventeenth and nineteenth centuries, the law did not change until 1925.[108] Meanwhile the practice of partible inheritance amongst male co-heirs could be found amongst the peasantry. It was also practised amongst small landowners during the nineteenth century, facilitating the spread of new capital.[109] Partible inheritance did nothing to challenge the masculinised construction of property relations. By dividing property between several men, rather than concentrating it in the hands of one man, it consolidated its establishment. Women of all classes, meanwhile, were affected by the law of coverture which enabled a husband to exercise control over his wife's property.

I have argued that the structure of property relations before capitalism made 'good sense' in terms of the protection of class and family interest. I have also shown how the system gave men a privileged position over women. Consider now the implications of the transition to capitalism where there is a much more explicit equation between the rights of individuals and property – and indeed the moral worth of individuals and property. Overall, in my view, this historical conjuncture contributed to the emergence of the ideology of the male breadwinner. This was played out amongst the propertied and the propertyless alike.

During the nineteenth century, for example, the idea of female domesticity, underpinned by the ideology of the male breadwinner, became prevalent amongst the middle classes. Female dependency thus construed was deemed a mark of social *and moral* standing, both of the woman herself and the family. More especially, the social and moral standing of individual men, as heads of household and family, was elevated.

The nineteenth century also witnessed the mobilisation of the ideology of the male breadwinner around demands for a 'family wage', i.e. an income sufficient for a husband to support his wife and children. The significance of the family wage for feminist analysis has been hotly debated. Some arguments suggest that the family wage system should be seen as the reconstitution of kin relations. Humphries, for example, sees it as providing a non-degrading form of support for non-labouring members of the working class, in the absence of the welfare state. At the same time she argues that it gave the working class a leverage through the supply of labour, enabling it to resist falls in the value of labour power. Thus, she believes, it was conducive to the development of a militant class consciousness amongst workers.[110]

Barrett and McIntosh, meanwhile, suggest a *coincidence* of interests between the capitalist class and a patriarchally-structured working class. They point out that the extraction of absolute surplus value during the nineteenth century was incompatible with the reproduction of the working class. They argue that it was imperative for capital, and indeed for labour, that the life and health of the working-class be protected. There was thus a common interest between the bourgeois state and the bourgeois philanthropists on the one hand and the working-class movement on the other. This was manifest in the Factory Acts of the 1840s, limiting the length of the working day, and protective legislation, such as the 1842 Mines Act, excluding women from work at the pit face.[111]

More recently Brenner and Ramas have argued that the material basis for the family wage system was rooted in the biological realities of reproduction in nineteenth-century conditions. They argue that, under capitalism, pregnancy, childbirth and lactation are not readily compatible with a production process increasingly separated from the household. Because of the threat to the rate of profit, capital was unwilling to lay out the necessary expenditure to overcome this through forms of maternity care. They conclude that 'historically developed capitalist class relations of production, in combination with the biological facts of reproduction, set up a powerful dynamic toward the family-household system, assuring women's continued subordination to men and their exaggerated vulnerability to capitalist exploitation'.[112]

Whatever position is adopted within these debates, we still need a much broader historical perspective than the one found in existing studies: i.e. one which focuses on the nineteenth century, to account for the ideology of the male breadwinner. We surely need to look back to historically specific forms of property and the implications for gender relations of a change in such forms.

Moreover, if demands for a family wage were a real, rather than a rhetorical, representation of re-created kin relations, and thus a defensive construct of a dispossessed class, such demands do not prevent us concluding that the concept of the male as breadwinner served to structure individualism along the lines of gender. In that concept, both male domination and the need of individualism were expressed.

By this I do not mean that the transition from feudalism to capitalism restructured gender relations in such a way as to lay the basis for the development of patriarchy *as an autonomous system* – relative or otherwise. In my view historical evidence shows that gendered class relations have been part of a single process. The fissuring and fractionalisation of class along the lines of gender, both in and through the ideology of the male breadwinner, which has often entailed the adoption of chauvinistic and sexist attitudes, may at the level of surface appearances lend itself to theories which posit separate systems of class and gender. However, this division needs to be understood in terms of the long historical and *masculinised* structuring of property relations, and the implications of this in the transition from feudalism to capitalism.

Although that transition may have restructured property relations more explicitly along the lines of gender, in my opinion it also created possibilities for *challenging* male privilege. The separation of the direct producers from the means of production forced the vast majority of the English population, men *and* women, into waged labour. But the relationship of labour and capital is founded upon conflict and contradiction. Wage labour is exploitative and, more often than not, unfulfilling. This fact provides a basis from which to challenge the social relations of labour and capital at the heart of capitalist society. The wage form also has subversive implications for gender relations. Although until 1870 men were entitled to keep their wives' wages,[113] the payment of wages to individuals regardless of sex provides at least an ideological basis to undermine equations between masculinity and property. (To what extent was the demand for a family wage system a reaction against this?)

In fact the development of absolute ownership rights vested in individuals threw up the possibility that *women* too, as individuals, could be absolute owners. There is no a priori reason in capitalist society that women as such be excluded from absolute ownership rights. That men have tended to acquire such rights more than women needs to be contextualised in terms of the long historical construction of masculinised property forms and the ideological implications of this.

This is not meant to imply that the development of individual property rights is necessary or sufficient to provide the basis for the liberation of women. It is clear that women have remained in a subordinate position in English society. It has already been suggested that the development of individual property rights laid the basis for divisions not only between but *within* social classes in English society. And, crucially, capitalist society has as its very foundation the fact that the vast majority of the population, women *and* men, lack access to and control over productive property.

However, the structures of capitalist property relations are shot through with contradictions. Individualised property rights throw up the possibility that property might be vested in *women* as *individuals*. In the sixteenth century, following the law of Separate Estate, whenever property was vested in a trustee for the personal maintenance of a married woman, she could enforce the application of the property without her husband's intervention. The Equity ruling also enabled a married woman to sue without her husband's intervention, but not, for some time, to sue against him.[114] The doctrine of Separate Estate could be used to keep property within a woman's natal kin group. It could thus be used, for example, to prevent a husband gaining access to the property of a heiress. It is likely, then, that the main intention of the Equity ruling was the protection of class and family interests. However the Married Women's Property Act of 1832 recognised individual rights of women.

And, of course, the pursuit of individual rights is one of the ideals which is embodied in much contemporary feminist pursuit of equal opportunities. But the limits of this approach lie in the very structure of capitalist property relations which throw up such ideological possibilities. The reality of capitalist social relations ultimately precludes the possibility of the vast majority of women *and* men having access to and control over productive property.

Chapter 5

From 'The Law of the Father' to 'capitalist fraternity'?

FROM 'THE LAW OF THE FATHER' ...

'The Law of the Father', a term used by Freudian and Lacanian psychoanalysts,[1] has been adapted by a number of feminist scholars to describe 'traditional' patriarchy, by which they mean the form of patriarchy prevalent in pre-capitalist societies. Carole Pateman uses it in this sense in her analysis of Sir Robert Filmer's work *Patriarcha* (1644),[2] a text written in defence of monarchical power in England. To what extent is it accurate to characterise forms of political power and office in feudal England as 'The Law of the Father'?

According to Peter Laslett,

> The value of *Patriarcha* as a historical document consists primarily in its revelation of the strength and persistence ... of ... the patriarchal attitude to political problems. It was because of patriarchalism that Sir Robert Filmer was read ... for in appealing to the power of the father and the relevance of the family to the state he touched the assumptions of his own readers and most of Locke's.[3]

In opposition to the contract theorists' assertion and defence of the rights and liberty of *sons*, Filmer upholds the political right of *fathers*. To uphold the right of kingship Filmer invokes Divine Will coupled with the age differentials which underpinned the law of primogeniture. All title to rule originated in the divine grant of kingly right to Adam. Adam was the first father, and political right derives from fatherhood. The historical development of nation states was seen by Filmer as a process of descent from Adam, the first father and supreme patriarch, who divided up the world between his sons, sons who in turn became fathers and patriarchs.[4]

Pateman, though claiming to be critical of radical feminist accounts, declares that her work has 'been prompted by writers customarily labelled radical feminists . . .'.[5] Against Filmer, Pateman argues that:

> The genesis of political power lies in Adam's conjugal or *sex right*, not in his fatherhood . . . [my emphasis]. If Adam was to be a father, Eve had to become a mother, and if Eve was to be a mother, then Adam must have sexual access to her body. In other words, sexual or conjugal right must *necessarily precede* the right of fatherhood.[6]

Pateman notes,

> Filmer makes it clear that Adam's political right is originally established in his right as a husband over Eve: 'God gave to Adam . . . the dominion over the woman', and 'God ordained Adam to rule over his wife, and her desires were to be subject to his.[7]

She quotes Filmer: 'here we have the original grant of government, and the fountain of all power placed in the Father of all mankind'. She recalls that in the Book of Genesis, where Eve is created only after Adam:

> [actually], she is . . . created. . . . from Adam, who is thus in a sense her parent. Filmer is able to treat all political right as the right of a father because the patriarchal father has the creative powers of both a mother and a father . . . he is *the* parent. . . . His procreative power . . . creates and maintains political right.[8]

Unfortunately, although Pateman alerts us to underlying patriarchal assumptions in Filmer's work, she does not address, any more than Filmer does, the actual historical processes involved in the formation of political power. Although an analysis of the origins of political power is beyond the scope of this study, the processes involved were far more complex than either divine will or sex right. We have only to *glance* at the history of state formation in England to appreciate this.

State formation was well under way in Anglo-Saxon society. By the tenth century much of the country had been unified under

King Edgar. Historian Steven Bassett suggests two ideal-type processes in the formation of Anglo-Saxon kingdoms: the 'take-over by an outside group of an existing territory in the early post-Roman period'[9] and

> the steady coalescence of adjacent settlement areas, a process accompanied by the translation of the leaders of dominant tribes into kings. This will have been well advanced long before the end of the Migration Period, though at different rates of speed in different areas; and it could no doubt have begun long before there were Anglo-Saxons in the area.[10]

The latter process 'proposes that kingship is likely to have evolved in many instances through the development of increasingly hierarchical leadership within the larger extended families'.[11]

Evidence from the Anglo-Saxon period, discussed in my previous and following chapters, demonstrates tendencies towards male domination within kinship organisation. However, this does not establish that male domination was the basis for the subsequent development of property structures and class relations. On the contrary, it seems to me that it suggests that kinship, gender and property were *symbiotic* and fundamental to the development of the English state.

Filmer himself had something to say about property and political power. Laslett paraphrases:

> Adam had been given possession of the whole world and everything in it, indeed it had been created for him to possess and to do with just as he wished. So Adam's eldest son had enjoyed during Adam's lifetime just as much property as Adam had voluntarily given him. After Adam's death *he inherited all his property as he inherited all his power. So* it was with all Adam's other sons, only they had no right to inherit any of Adam's property and had to be content with what their father or elder brother had voluntarily given them. So it was with all men who had existed since Adam: they had absolute right to just that property which they had lawfully inherited or which had been alienated to them by those who had likewise lawfully inherited it. . . .[12] (my emphasis)

So does Filmer offer us a metaphor applicable to the working of political power in feudal England? To some extent he does. Both before and after the Norman Conquest the exercise of institutionalised political power was dependent on the allocation of land by the monarch. During the Anglo-Saxon period thegns were rewarded with land and control over labour in return for military and administrative duties such as the collection of taxes.[13] Following the Norman Conquest most of England was divided up into large estates held from the Crown by a ruling minority of barons. These estates were *fiefs*,[14] a stipendiary tenement granted in return for military duty (later commuted into 'shield money') for the king. Principal vassals were obliged to hold a prescribed number of knights constantly at the king's disposal. Baronial estates could thus be parcelled out or subdivided into knights' fees. Marc Bloch points out that

> in many cases the same man occupied a dual role – as dependant of a more powerful man and a protector of humbler ones . . . a vast system of personal relationships whose intersecting threads ran from one level of the social structure to another.[15]

Within this complex social hierarchy every man was the 'man' of another 'man'.[16] But the king was lord of all lords.

Women were held incapable of bearing arms.[17] A straightforward biological explanation works here. Women did not enter into patron–client relations involving military service because of the realities of biological reproduction. By this I do not mean that biology was the *cause* of women's oppression. I mean that under certain social conditions, military feudalism being one of them, biological difference between women and men becomes socially significant. Discussing forms of citizenship, Carole Pateman points to

> older traditions in which citizenship has involved a distinctive form of activity and has also been closely tied to the bearing of arms. Feminist scholars are now showing that from ancient times there has been an integral connection between the warrior and conceptions of self identity and masculinity, which have been bound up with citizenship. . . .[18]

This legacy must surely have contributed to more modern but nonetheless (as we shall see) patriarchally structured conceptions of citizenship. Pateman cites Enoch Powell MP in a debate in 1981 on the British Nationalist Bill. Powell took the view that women should not pass on citizenship because 'nationality in the last resort is tested by fighting'.[19]

However, if disqualification of women on grounds of their presumed incapability of bearing arms was based on 'sex right' or was patriarchal *intent*, the question arises why the dominant political institution of feudal Europe – lordship and servitude – did not, while it was at it, disqualify women from receiving vassal homage. Women were in practice capable of inheriting fiefs. They could get their husbands to carry out the services of the fief and levy requisite services from lesser knights within the barony.[20] Nor were upper-class women ever deemed incapable of exercising authority. Feudal lords were not merely property owners but suzerains who enjoyed jurisdiction over their serfs and tenants. Upper-class women could hold ordinary fiefs and vast lands, and exercise, in their own right, the seigniorial powers that went with this.[21] Similarly, the evidence of wills, charters and Domesday Book shows that it was by no means abnormal for a woman to be lord/lady in charge of an estate in the pre-conquest period.[22]

As Marc Bloch says, 'no one was disturbed by the spectacle of the great lady presiding over the baronial court, when her husband was away'.[23] Similarly Kelly-Gadol points out that

> women also exercised power during the absence of warrior husbands. The lady presided over the court at such time, administered the estates, took charge of the vassal services due the lord. She *was* the lord, albeit in his name rather than her own – unless widowed and without male children.[24]

The Paston women of the fifteenth century also provide famous examples of women who administered or defended estates (often when their husbands were occupied in the King's service), long after the military system had declined.[25]

Nor was it impossible for women of the middle ranks to exercise a degree of political influence as independent guild members[26] and 'wives to men in the merchant and banking guilds that controlled the trade, the finances, and usually the political life of the town ...'.[27] Even propertyless women were not necessarily politically passive. In the late Middle Ages English peasant women sometimes led the peasantry's successful struggle against the nobility, and in so doing secured a certain amount of autonomy.[28] They could also take an active part in the manorial courts and be fined if they did not attend jury service.[29]

Indeed the role of women in the manorial courts, through which feudal lords holding land from the Crown exercised jurisdiction over the peasantry, was considerably better than that of the royal courts. According to Filmer, the common law, through which the political autonomy or 'parcelisation of sovereignty' in town and country was subject to the superior jurisdiction of the royal courts, was an exercise of fatherly will.

During the early part of the twelfth century, three distinct systems of law had operated in England: the Danelaw, the Law of Mercia and the Law of Wessex; within each, variations existed between counties. However, although some local variation continued throughout the feudal period, the customs of the king's court became dominant. The administration of the common law, in fact moved 'out of court', as a specialised institution independent of the king's immediate household.[30] Whilst Westminster became the seat of common law jurisdiction, itinerant justices toured England in circuits of the assize, which acted not only as courts of law but also, effectively, as a form of mobile government. By a statute of 1388, JPs were required to 'hold sessions of the peace' – the quarter sessions which began to replace county courts as the governmental and administrative authorities of the shires.[31]

Predictably, there is little to suggest that it was normal for women to act as judges or itinerant justices in the king's courts, nor for that matter as sheriffs with whom the execution of major judicial powers had previously lain.[32] Nor does it appear to have been usual for women to act as jurors in the king's courts.[33]

Pauline Stafford has discussed the way in which the development of a bureaucracy, separate from the king's household, reduced the political and administrative role of royal women.[34] Of some relevance here, perhaps, is a point to which anthropologists draw attention: that, historically and cross-culturally, long-distance trade has often been a male preserve.[35] But in my opinion a – if not *the* – crucial factor in explaining the absence of women from the administration of the common law in feudal England must have been the patriarchal structure of property relations. According to a statute of 1439, Justices of the Peace were eligible for office provided they possessed land and tenements with a value of 20 per annum.[36] We have already discussed at length why the bulk of strategic property was held by men in feudal England. The 'country gentleman commissioned by the king'[37] to administer the common law would indeed most likely be country gentlemen: the patriarchal structure of property relations saw to that.

Did the English common law system, then, as Filmer contends, uphold the Crown's 'fatherly' power? As Baker points out:

> Compared with the rest of Europe, England and its common law were precocious. The system of writs ... and the attendant procedure and terminology, the developed notion of pleas of the Crown with all the machinery for the discovery and trial of criminals, the existence of central and itinerant royal courts capable of subjecting the whole nation to the king's law and government – all these things were unique to England.[38]

The development of a nationally unified system of law in England certainly limited the parcelisation of sovereignty characteristic of other European feudal polities, indicating '. . . the declining power of feudal lords individually *vis-à-vis* the Crown, if not as a class *vis-à-vis* the peasants'.[39] However, one of the distinguishing features of English feudalism was the fusion between the monarchy and nobility at the local, judicial and administrative level. In the feudal societies of continental Europe the court system was divided between royal and seigniorial jurisdictions. In England the two were blended together. This prevented the development of professionalised royal justice as well as extensive baronial *haute justice*. Instead an unpaid aristocratic self-administration emerged in the counties.[40] This meant that for the execution and administration of the common law the English monarch actually depended upon the collaboration of the upper classes.[41] Whilst acting in the King's name they could also advance their own interests. They exercised miscellaneous governmental and police powers. For instance, from the mid-fourteenth century, after the labour crisis following the Black Death, they could fix the legal rate of wages at which labourers were compelled to work.[42]

Earlier, the power of feudal barons in England had been expressed in Magna Carta (1215), which marks the beginning of statute law. The king's power was circumscribed through definitions of its proper exercise: 'No free man shall be taken, or imprisoned or disseised, or outlawed, or exiled, or in any way ruined, except by lawful judgement of his peers or by the law of the land'.[43] For Filmer, the ultimate monarchist, such limitation would seem superfluous: he asserts that tyranny was not possible because the Crown exercised its monarchical power in a fatherly manner. For Filmer, Laslett says:

> The whole mechanism of the constitution existed to enable the king to exercise his absolute and arbitrary power in a fatherly way ... The fatherly nature of his power and the content of the Divine Law made it imperative that the king should do his utmost to preserve his subjects and to consult their benefit. That was why he had allowed in England the growth of good laws and good customs, that was why he had assembled Parliaments.[44]

How far did Filmer's ideological stance correspond to the realities of monarchical power in England? The English Crown has been seen as 'the strongest medieval monarchy in the West'.[45] There is much to support this view. The Norman and Angevin dynasties 'created a royal state unrivalled in its authority and efficiency'.[46] Whereas continental Europe featured semi-independent territorial potestates, Norman feudalism was administratively centralised.[47] Though the authority of the crown had been undermined during the War of the Roses, by the early sixteenth century Henry VII was able to restore and strengthen its position.[48] So much so in fact that Perry Anderson considers that the Tudor dynasty had made a 'promising start towards the construction of an English absolutism by the turn of the sixteenth century'.[49] The reign of Henry VIII did much to augment royal authority. The Reformation was an important part of that process. The move from the Universal Church of Rome to the Church of England, was, according to Loades 'undoubtedly the greatest single augmentation which royal authority has ever received'.[50] Not only did this give the Crown extended opportunities for patronage and control over extensive apparatus of propaganda through the pulpit, and moral regulation through the church courts,[51] but 'Henceforth the king would be addressed not as "Your Grace", a form of address which he shared with archbishops and dukes, but as "Your Majesty", a unique being exalted above all others in both church and state.'[52]

English monarchs often used Parliament to further their own interests. Edward I used Parliament as an instrument of royal government, thus reflecting the king's strength.[53] Henry VII actually discarded Parliament – it met only once during the last twelve years of his reign.[54] Henry VIII, though, actually used Parliament to mobilise the landed classes behind him in his dispute with Rome, securing its endorsement of the English state's political seizure of the church.[55] Perry Andersen observes:

> Henry VIII's use of Parliament, from which he expected and received few inconveniences, was confidently legalistic in approach: it was a necessary means to his own royal ends. Within the inherited framework of the English feudal polity, which had conferred singular powers on Parliament, a national Absolutism was in the making that in practice seemed to bear comparison with that of any of its continental counterparts.[56]

However, Parliament also acted as a counterweight to the power of the Crown. English medieval kings never in fact secured the relative legislative autonomy enjoyed by other European monarchs.[57] Parliament became recognised as the proper source of consent to taxation. Its assent also became essential to the development of legislation. Effectively, Parliament became a political assembly in which barons could oppose the king.[58] Moreover, not only was the English Parliament 'Singleton'[59] in nature, coinciding with the geographical boundaries of the country rather than a particular province – it was also 'conglomerate':[60] 'By the standards of the time, the English Parliament was unusually representative – of, at least . . . the political nation'.[61] It was not, as in the rest of Europe, divided internally along estate lines, i.e. those who pray (clergy), fight (nobles) and work (burghers). Knights, 'towns', barons and bishops sat alongside each other from an early date. (The two-chamber system of Lords and Commons which emerged during the fifteenth century actually marked an intra-class division within the nobility, rather than a division within Parliament along Estate lines.[62]

The Tudor dynasty may well have made 'a promising start towards the construction of an English absolutism'.[63] However, as Corrigan and Sayer point out, Henry VIII certainly 'knew what he was talking about when in 1543 he said "we at no time stand so highly in our estate Royal as in the time of Parliament" '.[64] Because government in the Tudor period was developed through Parliament and statute it 'was done at the cost of *limiting* the personal power of the monarch'[65] (my emphasis).

Given the male-dominated structure of property relations it is hardly surprising that it was predominantly 'sons' who were able thus to limit the power of the 'father', rather than 'daughters'.

Expressing contemporary fact and opinion, Glanville in the thirteenth century wrote that women 'are not able, have no need to, and are not accustomed to serving the lord, the king, either in the army or in any other royal service'.[66] If this had been *simply* because of the patriarchal structuring of property relations in medieval England, we might expect to find legislation explicitly banning female property holders from participating in the parliamentary process. Yet there was none. An Act of 1429 limited the franchise not to males but to forty-shilling freeholders.[67] The vast majority of women *and* men in England at this time were without sufficient property to qualify on these grounds, and thus excluded from the 'political nation'.

It is clear that women from the propertied classes could and did become involved in the exercise of political power through which the vast majority of other women *and* men were subordinated. For example, eleven peeresses were summoned to Parliament under Edward III. In 1277 four abbesses were summoned to Parliament, as was the Abbess of Shaftesbury and other abbesses in 1306.[68] There is also evidence of female participation in the election of members of Parliament. In 1412, for example, the indentures of the election of the Knights of the Shire for Yorkshire were sealed by various barons, the Archbishop of York, and Lucia, Countess of Kent. Similar indentures survive for 1415 with the writ of various nobles and that of Margaret, wife of Henry Vavarow, Chevalier. Women's seals also appear on indentures for Yorkshire between 1421 and 1429.[69] According to Statute 25 Edward I, parliamentary rights were given to women as well as men in the towns.[70] In the later part of the sixteenth century the Boroughs of Gatton (1554–5) and Aylesbury (1571–2) were owned by women and in both cases MPs were returned by them.[71] In legal cases during the reign of James I it was stated that if a *femme sole* had a freehold she could vote.[72] If access to political power and office had been intentionally patriarchal at this juncture, then surely it would have been logical for men to exclude women altogether?

Indeed, whilst it may be useful, with these qualifications I have suggested, to characterise the pre-capitalist form of patriarchy in England as 'the law of the father', that 'law' did not disbar women from the exercise of political power, including even monarchical power. Neither Filmer's version of patriarchal right, nor the actual constitutional practice in England, excluded women from access to the throne. From Filmer's point of view, although women *were* inferior to men (elder sisters were inferior to younger brothers because women were inferior in all situations), in the event of failure in the male line and consistent with the principle of women as residual heirs, authority could be handed down through a female.[73] Pauline Stafford suggests that the institution of primogeniture reduced the role of noblewomen in succession disputes.[74] Nevertheless, it did not exclude women from succeeding to the throne.

Motivated by a desire to resurrect women, particularly so-called 'great' women, in history, feminists have sometimes celebrated the political power and prestige of such women. This ignores the fact that their position derived from immense privilege in a highly stratified society, within which the vast majority of the population – women and men – were subordinated. As Coontz and Henderson recognise:

> The presence of powerful women ... is perfectly compatible with a general devaluation of womanhood ... noble women of the ruling class could and did exercise unprecedented power over both men and women below them even though – and indeed because – they were subordinate to their fathers or husbands. ...[75]

One example also pertinent to our discussion of the Crown's relationship to Parliament, should suffice to make the point. During the reign of Elizabeth I, the prestige and authority of the Crown – already strengthened under the Tudors – was greatly enhanced. Scotland had been linked to the English Crown, and the nation was both a prosperous European power with foreign allies and a bulwark of Protestantism.[76] Rebellion in Ireland was firmly put down, and Ireland was placed under English domination, with the power of the old clan system in ruins.[77] As England's monarch for nearly half a century, Elizabeth made a formidable contribution to the construction and consolidation of class power, through which the vast majority of the English population were subordinated.

The Elizabethan era saw the glorification, indeed deification, of the monarchy. In paintings, woodcuts, medals, sculpture and poetry, Elizabeth was hailed and likened to women of classical or biblical renown – Asnea, Judith, Deborah, Ceres, Cynthia, etc.

For both Protestants and Catholics Elizabeth replaced or at least rivalled the Virgin Mary.[78]

Rather than challenging the ideology of female subordination, however, Elizabeth I effectively furthered it. Alison Heisch has argued that throughout her reign Elizabeth continually presented herself as an exceptional woman, and thereby reaffirmed ideas of the weakness and frailty of women in general, and their inability to govern. For example, when referring to herself in terms of her gender, she highlights weakness and modesty:

> I cannot attribute these hopes and good successe to my devyse, without detracting mouche from the Divine Providence; nor challinge to my private commendation what is onlie dew to Go(o)ds eyernal glorie. My sea permits it not.[79]

and

> The weight and greatness of this matter might cawse in me some feare to speak, and bashfulness besides, a thing appropriate to my sex ... But yet the princely seate and kingly throne, wherin God (though unworthy) hath constituted me maketh thes two causes to seme little in myne eyes, though grevous perhaps to yor eares, and boldeneth me to say somewhat in this matter.[80]

and the now famous

> I know I have the body of a wek and feeble woman, but I have the heart and stomach of a king, and of a king of England too.[81]

Such pronouncements could be interpreted as skilful political manoeuvring on the part of Elizabeth, as skilful politician she no doubt was. The effect, nonetheless, would have been to sustain ideologies of female subordination.

As Heisch says, this did not protect Elizabeth from patriarchal opposition. She points out for example that Elizabeth was faced with a barrage of demands as to her intentions regarding marriage, in the process of which she was threatened with refusal to vote on the subsidy bill. Not only were members of her own privy council involved in this, but the tone of such petitions was patronising and paternal. Heisch suggests that such tactics would have been unthinkable in Henry VIII's reign. However, in her eagerness to identify the source of Elizabeth's problems as patriarchal, Heisch alludes to[82] but fails to develop the implications of the Crown's position *vis-à-vis* Parliament and the propertied classes at that time.

The Tudor monarchy had initially sponsored the gentry as a counterweight to the peerage. However, their growing political influence and prosperity (they had, for example, benefited significantly from the royal sale of church lands), was more and more an obstruction to the Crown. Parliament, which was summoned only thirteen times during forty-five years of Elizabeth I's reign, was becoming increasingly critical of government policy. Moreover, unlike its counterparts in Europe, the Tudor monarchy lacked a standing army. At the turn of the sixteenth century every English peer was a bearer of arms. By Elizabethan times only half the aristocracy had any experience of fighting. Just before the English Civil War most of the nobility had no military background at all.[83] An important consequence of this was that the English aristocracy switched to commercial activities long before their European counterparts.

Filmer's defence of royal power, 'the law of the father', against the claims of both aristocracy and democracy was made precisely when the power of the Crown was being challenged. But it was made in vain. The execution of King Charles in 1649 and the Glorious Revolution of 1688 were acute symptoms of the power of the capitalist classes which had, as we have seen, long been growing with the English social structure and polity. The act of 'parricide' also marked a transition to a new gender order.

... TO CAPITALIST FRATERNITY?

According to Pateman

> A contract between free and equal brothers replaces the 'law of the father' with public rules which bind all equally ... the rule of one man (father) is incompatible with civil society, which requires an impartial, impersonal set of rules promulgated by a collective body of men, who stand to the law and each other as free equals, as a fraternity. ...[84]

Discussion of women's exclusion from political rights and office in England has tended to focus on the nineteenth and early twentieth centuries, received opinion being that 'the 1832 Reform Bill made their exclusion from political citizenship explicit for the first time . . .'.[85] Little or no attention has been paid to the fact that moves in that direction had already begun with the political upheavals of the *seventeenth* century.

In 1621 protests were made against women exercising their choice at the election for Westminster and for the Long Parliament of Worcester. In 1628 in Knaresborough, an attempt was made to use the votes of widowed burgage holders, but the bailiff refused to admit them. Half a century later it was resolved before the poll that widows were to be disqualified. There was similar uncertainty in 1640 at the Suffolk election of the Long Parliament where the votes of widows were rejected by the Sheriff.[86] Four years later, the fourth part of Coke's *Institutes* was published, in which (with reference to the Proctors of the Clergy having a voice in Parliament) he stated:

> In many cases multitudes are bound by Acts of Parliament which are not parties to the election of Knights, citizens and burgesses as all they have no freedom, or having freehold in ancient dem . . . and *all women having freehold or no freehold and men within the age of one and twenty years.*[87] (my emphasis).

In a dispute in 1735 concerning whether or not women could vote for the office of sexton, Coke's fourth *Institute*, excluding women from the parliamentary franchise, was cited.[88] Then in 1739 it was decided that women could vote for the office of sexton on the grounds that it would not extend to another office and that the case could be considered a *private thing*.[89] In 1788 a decision was taken at the St Pancras vestry that women were not to vote for parish offices.[90]

Steinen writes that although women were enmeshed in the social relations of patronage which dominated eighteenth-century political and economic life from court to constituency, any *parliamentary* influence women may have had can only have been through men.[91] De facto of course this may not have been that much different from the medieval period. But by the eighth century attempts to exclude women had been openly articulated.

Even radical elements during the Civil War seem to have omitted women from citizenship. Although Lilburn of the Levellers had proclaimed 'all and every particular and individual man and woman were by nature all equal and alike in power, dignity and authority and majesty, none of them having by nature any authority, dominion or magisterial power on or above another',[92] the Levellers never advocated female suffrage. The *Leveller Petition of Women*, 1645, asserted the spiritual equality of women and men, a mutual interest in liberty and securities of law, but it did not go so far as to claim equal political rights for women.[93]

Winstanley of the Diggers expressed the view that women and men were equal, neither having the right to rule over the other.[94] However, in his *Law of Freedom*, where he upholds the family as the basic unit of society, and the elective principle is preserved, the commonwealth's officer is the father. The parish is a bigger family, a federation of households. The kingdom is a federation of parishes.[95]

In the *nineteenth* century, as Diana Leonard Barker says, 'The dominant interpretation of Individualist philosophy ... would be better named Familialism – or simply patriarchy. It envisaged full legal citizenship extended to all heads of households and "individual obligation" as being between household heads'.[96]

As Pateman puts it, there has been a 'long Western tradition in which the creation of political life has been seen as a masculine act of birth: as a male replica of the ability, which only women possess ...'. She points out that '... in Filmer's classic patriarchalism the father *is* both mother and father and creates political right through this fatherhood ...'. His argument, she says, is

that Adam's right of dominion over Eve is the right to become a father: a right to demand sexual access to Eve's body and insist that she give birth ... Eve's procreative, creative capacity is then denied and appropriated by *men* as the ability to give *political birth*, to be the "originators" of a new form of political order. ...

She sees the fraternal social contract as

a specifically modern reformulation of the patriarchal tradition. The father is dead, but the brothers appropriate the ability specific to women; they, too, can generate new political life and political right. The social contract is the point of origin, or birth of civil society, and simultaneously its separation from the private sphere of real birth and disorder of women. The brothers give birth to an artificial body, the body politic of civil society. ...

The 'birth' of the civil body politic however, is an act of reason, there is no analogue to a bodily act of procreation ... The natural paternal body of Filmer's patriarchy is metaphorically put to death by the contract theorists, but the 'artificial' body that replaces it is a construct of the mind ... the civil body politic is fashioned after the image of the male individual ... he is nothing more than a 'man of reason'. ...

Civil law encapsulates all that women lack. The civil law stems from a *reasoned* agreement that it is to the rational mutual advantage of the participants to the contract to constrain their interactions and desires through a law equally applicable to all. Women's passions render them incapable of making such a reasoned agreement or of upholding it if made. In other words, the patriarchal claim that there is a 'foundation in nature' for women's subjection to men is a claim that women's bodies must be governed by men's reason. The separation of civil society from the familial sphere is also a division between men's reason and women's bodies. The creation of the 'individual' presupposes the division of rational civil order from the disorder of womanly nature. ...[97]

Pateman's discussion comprises a powerful piece of metaphorical rhetoric, polemic even. But unfortunately it does not offer us very much in the way of explanation. *Why* was rationality and the notion of the political individual associated with *men* and not women? To answer this question we need to ask what the catalyst of this new gender order was? At the heart of the political upheavals of the seventeenth century lay a struggle between opposing classes for control of state power. The revolution symbolised by the execution – 'parricide' – of King Charles in 1649 and confirmed at the Restoration, ensured the development of capitalist social relations in England. We need not go into detailed analysis of the Civil War. It is sufficient for our purposes to note that, rather than clear-cut class divisions, 'historic blocs' of 'court' and 'country' played centre stage during the upheavals of the seventeenth century.[98]

To what extent was the exclusion of women from this new political order related to those conflicts? In a discussion of women and the franchise during this period, David Hirst suggests that social status may have had something to do with how much say women got. Although the answer was not always clear, '... when women of a lower social group were involved, questions began to be asked'.[99] To this we might perhaps add questions of political affiliation. Were such factors at work in the 1640 case where Royalists had accused the High Sheriff of Suffolk of partiality toward the Puritan candidates? The Sheriff cleared himself stating:

> It is true that by the ignorance of some of the clerkes at the other two tables, the oaths of some single women that were freeholders were taken without the knowledge of the said High Sheriff, who as soon as he had notice thereof instantly sent to forbid the same, conceiving it as a matter verie unworthie of any gentleman, and most dishonourable in such an election, to make use of their voices.[100]

To what extent was this dispute bound up with conflict between the historic blocs of 'court' and 'country'? At the heart of the 'country' bloc behind the overthrow of monarchical – fatherly – power were the magnates. They

> provided the realm with the most important part of that 'self-government at the King's command' which is the most significant trait of the English polity. They were the Deputy Lieutenants. They were the Sheriffs. They were J.Ps. They were the commissioners in the counties ... it was these same men who came to Parliament from the counties and the boroughs to make up the larger part of the membership of the House of Commons. This majority of local magnates seems to have increased right up to 1640, so that in the House of Commons of the Long Parliament all other groups appear as auxiliaries.[101]

It was these well-to-do classes, then, which were involved in the development and administration of the common law, a law which both upheld and countered the power of the monarch-'father'. What was at stake in the development of the common law was a theory and practice of *individualised rights*. Quotes from Milson highlight how this happened through the process of state formation and the concomitant development of private rights:

> For five centuries and more the relationship between landlord and tenant had been one of abstract rights fixed by the king's

courts. The tenant's rights had been independent of any discretion in the land. . . .[102]

. . . the relationship between *lord and* tenants was subjected to
the superior jurisdiction of royal courts and so became one of
reciprocal private rights rather than of dependent allocation . . .
The transfer of jurisdiction made abstract rights out of claims
to be allocated what was at the management's disposal, and
turned what were by nature customs of good management into
instant law.[103]

. . . what . . . the common law . . . did was . . . to develop sub-
stantive rules purporting to regulate in some detail how people
should behave, to analyse the relationship of life into a compre-
hensible system of rights and duties.[104]

By the time of the Restoration, common law had triumphed. It
was well adapted, by Coke, to the needs of embryonic capitalist
society.[105] Victorious over both the reforming demands of the
Levellers and the arbitrary intervention of the Crown, the
common law provided both stability and considerable liberty for
the propertied classes. For Coke, the common law was '*the
absolute perfection of reason*' (my emphasis).[106] We have already
seen that the 'collaboration of the well-to-do classes', through
which the common law developed, was, importantly in this context, a *male* collaboration.

In 1790 Heywood defined non-voters as those who lay under
natural incapacities and therefore could not exercise a sound
discretion, or were so much subordinated that they could not
have a will of their own in the choice of candidates.[107] This
definition of non-voters is very revealing of the nexus of individuality, rationality, civic status (property) and gender subordination.
*Owning property was the social prerequisite for having a will of
one's own.*

According to Macpherson, the Levellers seem to have taken it
for granted that women authorised their men to exercise their
political rights for them.[108] The Leveller position was one in which
government depended on *consent*, 'given, derived or assumed . . .
for the good benefit and comfort of each other and not for the
mischief, hurt or damage of any'.[109] This formula would cover an
assumed transfer of authority from women to their husbands. A

similar transfer of authority underlay the relationship of servant and master. According to Petty in the Putney Debate, servants were 'included' in their masters.[110]

As Diana Leonard Barker observes, 'The possibility of dependents (married women and children – and at an earlier date, servants) being seen as rational, contract-making, independent individuals was not considered in most political thought'[111] at the time.

Given all of this, it is really unsurprising that the new capitalist order was 'fraternal' in form. But what was the nature of this fraternity? Christopher Hill points out an

> inescapable ambiguity in the Puritan attitude towards authority. Authority in the state is analogous to authority in the family, but in the family the father's authority is absolute; ergo – authority in the state is that of all heads of households! The double-think recalls the Calvinist attitude to the Church as *both* the whole community *and* the elect only.[112]

As Hill sees it, this ambiguity corresponded to the social position of those who sought a greater degree of political influence for their class, but did not wish this to extend to 'full' democracy.[113]

The fraternity was a *class-specific* one; it excluded the vast majority of men as well as all women. *Property was the prerequisite for citizenship.* Thus for Locke, the philosopher and one of the founders of contract theory, political society was an association of free, equal, rational individuals capable of owning property. But he assumed class differentials among such individuals.

Pateman says,

> Both sides in the seventeenth-century controversy – unlike political theorists – were well aware that the new doctrine of natural freedom and equality had subversive implications for *all* relationships of power and subordination ... the contract theorists [with their] individualist language ... opened the thin ends of numerous revolutionary wedges, including a feminist wedge. ...[114]

Despite the individualist language of contract theory, however, it appears not to have occurred to Locke to consider women's participation in the founding of political society. There are several possible explanations of this omission. Locke may have confronted the question in the sections of his work which have been lost,[115] and we should bear in mind that Locke assumed class differentials among free, equal and rational individuals capable of owning property: a class differential could also have been a gender differential.[116] Melissa Butler writes:

> Locke was also a good enough propagandist to have realised how deeply ingrained patriarchalism was in everyday life . . . the audience Locke was addressing was essentially an audience of fathers, household heads and family sovereigns. Locke had freed them from political subjection to a patriarchal superior – the King. He did not risk alienating his audience by clearly conferring a new political status on their subordinates, that is, on women.[117]

More radically, Pateman sees Locke's 'individual' as masculine by definition.[118] In Locke's state of nature 'women are excluded from the status of "individual" in the natural condition . . . only men naturally have the characteristics of free and equal beings . . .'.[119] Wives are subject according to Locke because 'generally the Laws of mankind and customs of Nations have ordered it so; *and there is, I grant, a Foundation in Nature for it'*.[120] Women are natural subjects rather than free and equal 'individuals'.

In all of this, Pateman's radical-feminist assumptions cause her to miss an all-important point. The position in which she perceives (correctly) that women were left cannot be separated from the individualisation of rights basic to the process of state formation. Where individual legal subjects – citizens – are empowered by property, and property is, for all the reasons thus far outlined, overwhelmingly a male preserve, *state-regulated individualism*, rather than calculated disempowering of women as a category, provided the soil in which gender divisions were nurtured. The working out of *class* relations, notably around ownership as a condition of legal individuality, was basic in defining the parameters of women's access to political power within the state.

Of course, men did get much the best of the deal. Mary Wollstonecraft saw this two centuries ago, identifying male passion as responsible for the political subordination of women.[121] She perceived men as being 'governed by self-interest . . .'[122] Such self-interest could develop within the nexus of property, individuality, civic status and rationality. It was this complex set of social relations rather than 'male power' *per se* which served to structure and articulate political individualism along the lines of gender.

But for Locke the subjection of women was not political. Eve's subjection

> can be no other subjection than what every wife owes her Husband ... Adam's can be only a Conjugal Power, not Political, the Power that every Husband hath to order the things of private Concernment in his Family, as Proprietor of the Goods and Lands there, and to have his Will take place before that of his wife in all things of their common Concernment; *but not a Political Power of Life and Death over her*, much less over anybody else.[123]

Pateman comments that 'Locke's separation of paternal from political power' is such that 'the public sphere can be seen as encompassing all social life apart from domestic life ... private and public spheres are grounded in opposing principles ...'.[124]

This dichotomising of family and political life is quite different from earlier, organic, conceptions of family and state. In *Patriarcha*, for example, Filmer posits a homologous relationship between families and kingdoms. The family *was* political society. Everybody lived in families and therefore in political society.[125] The subordination of women is derived from Divine Right. For the earlier theorist Thomas Hobbes, too, the relationship between families and kingdoms was a homologous one: 'Cities and kingdoms ... are but greater families',[126] a great family is a kingdom, and a little kingdom a family,[127] and if the family

> grow by multiplication of children, either by generation, or adoption; or of servants, either by generation, conquest, or voluntary submission, to be so great and numerous, as in all probability it may protect itself, then is that family called a *patrimonial kingdom*. ...[128]

In contrast to Filmer, Hobbes does not, however, view the state as an extension of the family. Instead the state is the *model for* the family. In his system, the subordination of women arises through the marriage contract.[129] How, then, could Locke separate family and state and argue that the subordination of women was non-political? To answer these questions (which Pateman does not address) we need to bear in mind the fact that Locke was writing at the point of emergence of a new capitalist conception of the political, in which family and state, public and private had become distinct and separate spheres. Marx captures this well:

> *Feudalism* ... was *directly political*, that is to say, the elements of civil life, for example, property, or the family, or the mode of labour, were raised to the level of political life in the form of seigniority, estates, and corporations. ...[130]

Discussing this, Derek Sayer says:

> In feudalism, 'civil' and 'political', 'public' and 'private', coincided; indeed these very terms are anachronistic as applied to the medieval world, for such distinctions are precisely a product of bourgeois historical development. Individuals' 'civil' statuses were at the same time 'political' and it would be meaningless to try to differentiate between 'public' and 'private' at the level of institutions.[131]

This contrasts with capitalist society as analysed by Marx:

> Where the political state has achieved its true development, man – not only in thought, in consciousness, but in *reality* ... leads a twofold life ... life in the *political community*, in which he considers himself a *communal being*, and life in *civil society*, in which he acts as a *private individual*. ...[132]

Locke's categorisation of women's subordination within the family as non-political was not as misogynistic as a present-day feminist reading might take it to be. It was symptomatic of the reification of the 'political' in capitalist society: a development which, since women generally did not hold property and property was the prerequisite of citizenship, *per se* left women outside the political sphere. The reification coincided with a new form of patriarchal relations within the political order. Qualifications notwithstanding, the transition from feudalism to capitalism marked a transition from the law of the father to a capitalist fraternity.

Chapter 6

Sisters, daughters and subordinate wives

A useful – if at first slightly surprising – approach to understanding the position of women in the medieval English family historically can be drawn from Karen Sacks' study of African societies, *Sisters and Wives*. Sacks herself points out the parallels, suggesting that in pre-feudal Europe, as in twentieth century Africa, women may have held contradictory roles, equal as sisters, subordinate as wives. She also argues that class societies, 'to the extent that they developed from patri-corporations, transformed women from sister and wife to daughter and wife, making them perennial subordinates'.[1]

It will be my argument that women in Anglo-Saxon society could be sister, daughter and subordinate wife, all at the same time, becoming, by the post-conquest period, daughter and wife only. We shall see too that feudalism and capitalism have been associated with specific expressions of women's subordinate status as daughters and wives.

FROM SISTERS, DAUGHTERS AND SUBORDINATE WIVES ...

Anglo-Saxon women continued after marriage to belong to their own blood kindred.[2] This meant that legal responsibility for the actions of a married woman was borne by her and her kinsmen. This is demonstrable from the payment of wergild. Wergild had originally replaced blood feud as a way of resolving conflicts, and expressed both the unity of the kindred in paying for the crimes of their members and the justice of the accuser's case. However, with the development of private property wergild was converted into a fine paid by the accused *individual* to members of the victim's personal kindred. Where the victim was 'kinless' wergild was paid to the king or the victim's lord.[3] Under Alfred, if a pregnant woman was murdered, her wergild was calculated separately from that of her unborn child.[4]

Where a married woman committed murder, the *Leges Henrici* specify that the woman's blood relatives, not her husband, were to be penalised.[5] The fact of marriage did not implicate either husband or wife in the wrong-doing of the other: they did not form one unit of legal responsibility.[6] As Christine Fell points out, 'it is not as in some societies that women move from the authority of her father to that of her husband. On the contrary she retains within her marriage the support of her family'.[7]

The West Saxon King Ine (688–94) provides us with evidence of this: 'If a husband steals any cattle and brings it into his house ... if she declare with an oath that she did not taste of the stolen meat, she is to receive her third portion'[8] (i.e. if her husband's possessions were forfeit she would retain her due). In *Leis Wellelme* the property of a convicted thief is to be divided between his wife and his lord. Athelstan assigns a thief's wife, if not guilty, a third of his confiscated property.[9] Whitred, King of Kent in the seventh century, writes: 'if a man sacrifices to devils without his wife's knowledge he is liable to pay all his goods ...'.[10] During Cnut's reign in the eleventh century: 'And if any man brings home stolen property to his cottage ... unless it has been brought under the wife's lock and key she is to be clear'.[11] However, Ine states that 'if anyone shall steal, in such a way that his wife and children know nothing of it, he shall pay sixty shillings as fine: but if he steals with the knowledge of all his household they are all to go into slavery'.[12]

The fact that a woman's blood kindred remained collectively responsible for her crimes after her marriage illustrates at least an element of 'sisterly' relations in Anglo-Saxon kinship systems. Women's access to family property as heiresses and at their marriage can be interpreted similarly. But it might just as easily be interpreted as evidence of their 'daughterly' – subordinate – status: women usually inherited landed property as *residual* heirs and were, crucially, *dependent* upon their family – fathers in particular – for their marriage portions. Further, if a woman was murdered, compensation was made according to her *father's* wergild.[13] Evidence also suggests that parents – fathers – were exercising control over the choice of their daughters' (and sons') marital partners. Cnut, aware of this, emphasised the importance of consent: 'and no woman or maiden shall ever be forced to marry a man who she dislikes';[14] and Aethelred, while prescribing twelve months' celibacy for widows, adds: 'afterwards let her choose what she herself will'.[15] Yet laws against forced marriage were not always observed.[16] Indeed, attempts to regulate relationships actually suggest that women's freedom was often overridden.

What of the status of wives in relation to husbands? Even though husband and wife did not form one unit of legal responsibility in Anglo-Saxon society, husbands were clearly considered to have authority over their wives in most cases. Ine, for example, decreed that: 'if a husband steals a beast and carries it into his house and it is seized therein, he shall forfeit his share of the household property and his wife only being exempt because *she must obey her lord* . . .'.[17] Similarly, Whitred indicates that a man of the social class known as ceorl was a freeman, husband and *head of the family*.[18] According to Cnut 'no wife can forbid her husband to deposit anything he desires in his cottage'.[19]

How might we explain the existence of sisterly, daughterly and subordinate wife status for women in Anglo-Saxon society? Sacks argues that (a) women's contradictory position as sister and wife stems from corporate control of productive means, specifically through patricorporations (i.e. patrilineal and patrilocal kin corporations), and that (b) the transformation of women into perennial subordinates as daughter and wife is a consequence of the emergence of class society out of patricorporations.[20]

However, the system of kinship reckoning in Anglo-Saxon society makes it unlikely that communal tenure existed. In unilineal systems where descent and affiliation is traced through one parent rather than another, demarcated kin groups are formed which persist across generations. Anglo-Saxon kinship however was not unilineal but *bilateral*, descent and affiliation being traceable through both females and males. Bilateral sets of consanguineal kin centred on a focal relative (designated 'Ego' by anthropologists) have no structural persistence across generations. They have been likened to a series of overlapping circles.[21] In bilateral systems there is no continuity of possession: kin groups, as a whole, do not own anything. Where Anglo-Saxon wills show

land as being inalienable from the kin group, they mean that
the land bequeathed is to remain within a certain range of kin.
This by no means implies communal ownership.[22]

Nor was there any sign of patrinominal groups. Although the
names of children were sometimes compounded from the names
of parents there is no evidence of named kin groups as we would
today speak of 'the Smiths' or 'the Joneses'. This fact together
with the existence of 'Ego'-centred bilateral groups of kin con-
futes any assumption that Anglo-Saxon kinship was patrilineal.

However kinship remained an important organising principle
in society. There were important sets of rights and duties associated with kinship in Anglo-Saxon society. Rights included not
being overlooked as heirs of bookland. Duties included the
avenging of death and support in a feud or payment of wergild.
Such rights and duties functioned within a closely related set of
relatives. It is within such terms that we can account for the
'sisterly' status of women in the period.

If the 'sisterly' status of women in Anglo-Saxon society can be
explained thus, how might we account for the daughterly and
wifely subordinate status of women also? There does seem to
have been a certain emphasis on agnatic links and patrilateral
kin. This is apparent in the elaboration of terminology used to
denote ties of kinship, more terms existing for the male than for
the female side.[23] Where ancestry was traced through a single
line, it was usually done agnatically.[24] Paternal rather than
maternal kinsmen were usually appointed as a child's protectors.
According to King Alfred, if a man without paternal kin killed a
man, his maternal kin were to pay a third of the wergild. The
ratio of 2:1 is preserved in Athelstan's laws, where a man demand-
ing payment for a kinsman who has been killed was to be supported by two oath-givers from the paternal kin and one from
the maternal kin.[25] This does not mean that paternal kin were
twice as important as maternal kin. But it does mean that an
agnatic bias existed in some contexts.[26]

How should we interpret this agnatic patrilateral bias? The
elaboration of terms for male kin is not surprising in a society in
which a man's association with a lord, in war, administration and
economic life, was so fundamental.[27] The emphasis on patrilateral
kin was significant for a society in which physical force was at a
premium in battle and feud.[28] Patterns of residence also suggest
virilocal customs, a wife going to live with her husband upon

marriage.[29] Such factors doubtless bolstered the position of men in society, and, more specifically the position of husbands over wives. Further, Anglo-Saxon society was characterised by a complex interweaving of lordship and kinship. Although the claims of lordship could clash with those of kindred, with duty to one's lord becoming increasingly important, in actual fact one's 'lord' might very well be the head of one's kingroup.

We have seen too that there was an emphasis on the male line in the transmission of property. This made sense as a strategy to protect and further the interests of class and kinship. But it also bolstered the position of men and emphasised female dependency. It was interests of class and kinship, too, which dictated the exercise of control over choice of marital partner. Restrictions as to marriage choice can be seen as a method of ensuring that daughters did not marry too far 'down' or 'out'. It might also be a way of making political and economic alliances. 'Like marry like or better', Jack Goody writes. 'Fathers try to arrange the marriage of their daughters to men of equal or superior standing'.[30] Along with dowry, Goody sees 'in' marriage as a method of preserving differences of property. But the preservation of such differences fostered female, specifically 'daughterly', dependence.

To account for the existence of sisterly, daughterly and wifely relations of 'equality' and subordination in Anglo-Saxon times, then, we need to understand that kinship had a wider range of functions than is the case today. Importantly, these kinship structures expressed an agnatic and patrilateral bias. They also existed within a highly stratified society, one indicator of which was the presence of the social relation of lordship.

... TO DAUGHTERS AND SUBORDINATE WIVES ONLY

In contrast to the Anglo-Saxon period, in the post-conquest period husband and wife formed one unit of legal responsibility. Bracton, writing in the thirteenth century, cites a case in which a husband and wife were deemed to be jointly guilty of producing a forged charter. The husband was hanged, but she was freed on the grounds that she had acted under her husband.[31] This was of course similar to the Anglo-Saxon situation. Now, however, *husbands* rather than a woman's natal kin were liable for the debts or wrongs committed by their wives.[32] A wife's legal existence was suspended or incorporated into that of her husband.

During the sixteenth and seventeenth centuries in particular, political philosophers and Puritan ideologies often drew an analogy between family and state – an analogy, or metaphor, which could now be found enshrined in law. The law of Petty Treason, for example, established husbands as petty sovereigns – domestic monarchs. Treason, defined as a 'treacherous usurpation of or challenge to the king's authority' was the most serious offence known in English law. Petty Treason was a lesser form of the offence. Thus,

> There is another manner of treason, that is to say when a servant slayeth his Master or a *wife her husband* or a religious slayeth his prelate, *of whom he oweth faith and obedience*[33] (my emphasis).

The offence was not treated simply as murder. As a lesser form of treason it was more severely punished. Thus during the reign of Henry VII, a wife who killed her husband would be put to death by burning. The last such burning occurred in the eighteenth century, and the crime was not reclassified as murder until 1828.[34] Until the late sixteenth century Benefit of Clergy, i.e. the right to be tried in the ecclesiastical courts – where the death penalty could not be imposed – was a *male* privilege.[35]

We might also draw an analogy between a husband's right to chastise his wife and the state's use of force to discipline and punish subjects. Blackstone, writing in the eighteenth century, points out that

> The husband also (by the old law) might give his wife ... correction ... The civil law gave the husband the same or larger authority over his wife, allowing him for some misdemeanours, flagellis et sustibus acritor, for others only modicon.

According to the *Lawes Resolution of Women's Rights*, compiled during the Tudor period and published in 1632, 'The Baron may beate his wife.'[36]

How might we explain such ideological and legal enforcement of male authority? Historians Coontz and Henderson point out that

> the establishment of the individual household as the basic social unit of state society increased the power of the husband as the family's public representative and deprived women of a second

place of reference and refuge in their natal kin groups. The diffused authority that had allowed women in even patrilineal kinship societies to sometimes gain manoeuvring room between the spheres of the husband's and the father's authority was gone. Especially as the household began to be seen as a microcosm of the social order, male authority within the household was reinforced ideologically and even legally.[37]

How did the household become this 'microcosm of the social order' in England? Nuclear households were in fact delineated from wider kinship groupings at an early date. In Anglo-Saxon England the 'hide' defined a unit of land sufficient to support a man and his nuclear family. (In fact the hide is very ancient indeed. In James Campbell's graphic phrase, it is 'part of the grammar of Indo-European society'.)[38] It was through the processes of class and state formation that the wider significance and function of kinship as an organising principle of society was narrowed. That process was well under way in Anglo-Saxon times. The Normans and their successors built upon that foundation. One pertinent indicator of the destructive effect on kin-based organisation is that by the post-conquest period the juridical functions of kinship expressed in wergild had disappeared. As women were no longer supported through this mechanism by their natal kin groups, married women became instead dependent upon their husbands, who were now liable for their debts and wrongs. Increased emphasis on nuclear groupings would also make women's dependence upon an individual man – father or husband – for access to resources much more obvious. It is my argument, then, that as the nuclear family/household became more clearly separated from the wider kin group through the processes of class and state formation, any pre-existing tendency towards gender inequality would be exacerbated.

Particular moments during feudalism and state formation were also important for the elevation of male authority within the nuclear family/household. The Reformation, interpreted by some as an important component part of England's limited absolutism, and which, through the sale of church lands, was certainly significant in the development of capitalism, is a case in point. The nationalisation of the church – the shift from the Universal Church of Rome to the Church of England under monarchical supremacy – has, we have seen, been called 'the greatest single augmentation which royal authority has ever received'.[39] New conceptions of kingship were articulated in the king's address: no longer simply 'Your Grace', but now 'Your Majesty', exalted above all others in both church and state.[40] The metaphor between family/household and state persisted. According to Christopher Hill, for example, whilst the Reformation reduced the role of priests, it simultaneously elevated the authority of the head of household.[41] Royal supremacy greatly increased the Crown's opportunities for patronage and control of propaganda through the pulpit, and moral regulation through the ecclesiastical courts.[42] Church attendance was *compulsory*. By law heads of households were responsible for ensuring that their families attended Sunday service.[43]

State formation is of course intimately connected to class formation, and it is in terms of feudal class relations and the process of state formation that we can understand the law of Petty Treason. Whilst at the very least increasing the symbolic power of husbands *vis-à-vis* their wives, the enactment of the law needs to be understood in terms of the elevation of the *king's* power. We have already seen that patron–client relations, as manifest in the relationship of retainers to the king, were significant in the destruction of kin-based society and in the process of state formation in England. Indeed, the relationship of patron–client came to permeate the society. This is apparent in the law of Petty Treason itself, where the relationship of husband and wife is set alongside that of master and servant and prelate and religious. In this vein, discussing married women's property rights under feudalism, Alan Macfarlane notes that a married woman was a *femme coverte*, i.e. a 'covered woman'. He says that the image of a wife being covered was linked to that of the feudal tenant. A wife became a tenant or 'man' to her lord.[44]

However, we have seen that in England the *king* was lord of all lords. One important 'peculiarity' of England was the absence of seigniorial *haute justice* on the French model. Lords generally enjoyed jurisdiction over their unfree tenants through manorial courts. However, even this was circumscribed. They could not, for instance, exact the death penalty as some continental lords undoubtedly could and did. Where the death penalty was imposed for Petty Treason, it was done so as part of the king's law. Whilst the law did, even if only in symbolic terms, elevate the position of husbands *vis-à-vis* their wives, it was locked into a system of state power designed to maintain and further feudal *class* power.

Feminists sometimes assert that the position of married women historically has been one of slavery.[45] But the status of 'covered woman' was very different from that of complete absorption into her husband's identity. A 'covered woman' actually had an independence of her own, as did a feudal tenant.[46] Women were *expected* to obey their husbands (there is plenty of evidence which demonstrates that they did not meet this expectation), but this did not extend to disregard of state authority. Married women were accountable for the crimes of murder and treason.[47] Although Bracton had stated that as a general rule a wife should obey her husband, this obedience was not expected to extend to participation in criminal activities.[48]

The distinction between chastisement and violence is a moot point. Still, according to Blackstone, 'this power of correction [was] confined within reasonable bounds and the husband was prohibited from using any violence on his wife'.[49] In fact, according to the *Lawes Resolution of Women's Rights*, 'If a woman be threatened by her husband to be beaten ... sets down a writ which she may sue out of Chancery to compel him to find surety of honest behaviour'.[50] Of course the realities of class and gender divisions may well have militated against such litigation. And of course the confinement of chastisement 'within reasonable bounds' is itself indicative of a relationship of dominance and subordination.

But why should there have been any attempt at all to safeguard the interests of women? Bennett points out that neither sex was particularly advantaged by the legal responsibility of husbands for wives. As the public identity of wives was undermined, husbands could accrue onerous legal responsibilities as householders.[51] The position of husband as head of household was then intimately connected to state formation. The authority of husbands was both elevated and ultimately limited by state power.

Daughters, meanwhile, retained their status as subordinates. As in Anglo-Saxon times their access to family resources was circumscribed by the masculinised structure of property relations. Their freedom of choice as regards marital partners, too, was often limited. Amongst the nobility and gentry, freedom of choice was often circumscribed in the interests of land, money and rank.[52] The more prosperous urban burgesses were keen to arrange marriages for economic advantage.[53] Similarly, amongst the peasantry, fathers might look for a suitable match amongst men of their own social class and substance.[54] As far as villein women were concerned, if they married outside the demesne, the lord lost both the woman's labour and her potential reproductive capacities.[55] Meanwhile, if a widow did not have an adult son, a lord might argue that she was unable to provide labour services adequately. She might therefore be forced to marry, or move out.[56]

The state/household metaphor was also preserved. The Crown could and did interfere in the marriages of the propertied classes beyond its 'gift'. It might either reward favourites or actually obstruct marriages. Elizabeth I, for example, interfered frequently. She often tried to prevent marriages between her courtiers and women of the aristocracy, perhaps because of a desire to maintain the Court as a focus of interest for the upper classes. James I positively encouraged marriages, and as a supporter of union between Scotland and England, was especially favourable to Anglo-Scottish marriages.[57] The Crown's interests were also served by the system of wardship through which the Crown became the guardian of tenants-in-chief who inherited as minors. This enabled the Crown to arrange marriages to its own political and financial advantage. The practice enabled the Crown to keep a check over its feudatories.[58] To understand the survival of the practice long after the military system had ended, we need to consider the dynamics of class relations within feudal England. The Crown lacked modern revenue machinery to enable it to claim contributions towards the high costs of government. So, whilst the landed classes in the House of Commons resisted government demands for money, the Crown resorted to this method of indirect taxation.

However, by the end of the sixteenth century and beginning of the seventeenth century there was increasing criticism of the system of wardship. As part of 'fiscal feudalism', wardship had become one of the major rackets of Tudor England. At the beginning of the sixteenth century, classes from the peerage through to the yeomanry were liable to discover that they were sleeping-tenants-in-chief of the Crown.[59] Wardship endangered family fortunes and undermined the authority of parents. Abuses of the system were a frequent cause of complaint in the Commons. In the early seventeenth century emphasis shifted from abuses to the system itself. In 1646 the Court of Wards was abolished along with feudal tenures.[60] According to Lawrence Stone, as the Crown monopolised more of the profits for itself (rather than allowing peers and courtiers to prey upon and patronise the gentry), and as respect for individual freedom of choice began to be accepted, the overthrow of the court was inevitable.[61]

Indeed, Stone suggests that between 1660 and 1800 there was a conflict of ideals with respect to property marriage and marriage for reasons of romantic love.[62] He argues that it was this conflict of ideals that explains the popularity of Richardson's *Clarissa*, particularly amongst the bourgeoisie.[63] Similarly, Christopher Hill has argued that

> the social background to *Clarissa*, then, is this developing bour-
> geois society of which Richardson was part and parcel, and
> which was the main novel reading public. The aristocracy owed
> its continuing predominance in part to its concentration of
> family property by entail and marriages for money. Political
> compromise between aristocracy and bourgeoisie had been
> arrived at in the seventeenth century; but compromise in the
> realm of ideas was still being worked out. Richardson's
> novels ... are 'bourgeois art.[64]

> *Clarissa* represents the supreme criticism of property marriage.
> But in this it is a culmination of the Puritan tradition ... The
> rise of capitalism and Protestantism brought a new conception
> of marriage ... a companionship based on mutual affection.[65]

Amongst the aristocracy and squirearchy there does not seem to have been any single or simple pattern.[66] By the mid-eighteenth century there was both a series of county marriage markets and a national marriage market centred on London and Bath. To an extent these markets allowed sons and daughters greater freedom of choice (which apparently already existed lower down the social scale).[67] However, by providing potential spouses who would have the necessary financial and social qualifications, marriage markets allowed this degree of freedom of choice without threatening the long-term material interests of the family.[68]

In 1753 Lord Hardwick's Marriage Act made parental consent necessary in cases of marriage below the age of twenty-one. According to Trumbach the Act should not be interpreted as a reassertion of patriarchal power. He believes that parents were happy to see their children marry for love as long as they did not make precipitate decisions and did not entirely forget considerations of birth and wealth.[69] He also notes the outlawing of professional matchmakers in 1720 as an index of the decline of mercenary marriage.[70] Jacqueline Sarsby, however, has argued that the Act increased control over marriages and gives 'no indication of the new affection between parents and children, the absence of their previous mercenary interests, which Stone asserts for families in the upper ranks of eighteenth century society'.[71] 'The desire of the landed classes to preserve their inheritance intact is suggested by the growth in the proportion of peers' daughters who never married'.[72] Indeed, the wholesale commercialisation of the period, displacing older notions of rank through birth, may well have encouraged the wealthy and aspiring to become *more* rather than less 'mercenary'. The eighteenth century remained an extraordinarily (and for the most part openly) mercenary age, the effect of which may well have been to *increase* patriarchal power.

As far as the position of wives is concerned, I have already argued that the middle-class ideology of female domesticity, demands for a family wage and the explicit political disenfranchisement of women, all of which were associated with the development of capitalism, intensified patriarchal power. But I have also illustrated potentially subversive possibilities inherent in capitalist social relations. Such possibilities could provide women with a basis from which to challenge their subordinate status as daughters and wives.

In this chapter I have argued that we can characterise the position of women within the family in Anglo-Saxon times as both 'equal' sisters and subordinate daughters and wives. However, as the significance and function of kinship was undercut the position of women within the family can be more easily characterised as subordinate daughter and wife only. I have also indicated that particular periods during feudalism, and the development of capitalism, intensified that subordinate status. But capitalism has also generated contradictions sufficient at least to enable women to question and challenge that status.

Chapter 7

Women as property

A number of feminist writers have expressed the view that women in England have, historically, been treated as property; and they are backed up by some historians. To what extent is this contention valid? What is the evidence that has been used to support it?

We can start our examination with the laws relating to adultery – a crime with a strong connotation of property, the woman's body being illicitly given to a man other than its 'owner', her husband.

It is certainly the case that punishment of women guilty of adultery could be extreme. In the reign of Cnut, they stood to lose both nose and ears.[1] Alfred decreed: 'If anyone lies with the wife of a man whose wergild is 1200 shillings, he shall pay 120 shillings compensation to the husband; to a husband whose wergild is 600 shillings he shall pay 40 shillings compensation'.[2]

Feminist historian Nazife Basher considers that the prominence of rape in English statute law from Anglo-Saxon times until the sixteenth century 'was due to the law's concern with the protection of male property rather than to its concern with the welfare of women'.[3] What is the evidence to support this statement?

During the Anglo-Saxon period, King Aethelbert decreed:

> if a man lies with a maiden belonging to the King he shall pay 50 shillings compensation. If she is a grindling slave he shall pay 25 shillings compensation ... If a man lies with a commoner's serving maid, he shall pay 6 shillings compensation ... with a slave of the second class [he shall pay] 50 sceattas ... if with one of the third class 30 sceattas. ...[4]

Klink argues that such crimes were clearly regarded as having been committed against the guardian or master rather than the woman herself, since the fines for the violation of female slaves were graded according to the rank of the master.[5] Basher writes that, 'The language of medieval rape statutes defined rape and abduction interchangeably. Both involve the *theft* of a woman.' She cites Pollock and Maitland in support of her view:

> The crime which we call rape had in very old days been hardly severed from that which we call abduction; if it had wronged the woman, it had wronged her kinsmen also, and they would have felt themselves seriously wronged even if she had given her consent, and had, as we should say, eloped.[6]

Laws passed in the thirteenth century do indeed seem to bracket rape and abduction together. These laws and others enacted during the fourteenth and fifteenth centuries were designed to facilitate legal action by families, which might run counter to the desires of the woman herself. Thus, even if a woman connived in her own 'rape' – eloped – legal action could be taken against both the man and the woman by the woman's family. This action would often include debarring her from inheritance.[7]

There was a general link between property and the legal regulation of sexual behaviour. That such a relationship exists is widely accepted and will not be debated here. But I would like to highlight the pre-conquest period, where we can see the early establishment of this link. I shall then argue that the view that women themselves were property hinges on a historically specific concept of property, which is projected back into periods of history where no such concept yet existed. It is the failure of feminists and historians to recognise their own hindsight which leads them to assert that women themselves were property in the sense that, say, cows were.

In 'The Origins of the Family, Private Property and the State', Engels long ago alerted us to the connection between the development of private property, class society and the imposition of monogamy. Monogamy could ensure the legitimacy of heirs and facilitate the consolidation of estates.[8] There is little reason to suppose that the imposition of monogamy and the legal regulation of marriage both prior to and after the Norman Conquest functioned in any way other than this. In 746–7, Boniface and seven other bishops wrote to King Aethelbert of Mercia, urging him to take a wife:

For if the race of the English as is noised abroad throughout these provinces and is cast up against us in France and in Italy and is used as a reproach by the pagans themselves spurning lawful marriages, lives a foul life in adultery and lasciviousness, after the pattern of the people of Sodom it is to be expected that from such intercourse with harlots there will be born a degenerated people, ignoble, raging with lust.[9]

Christine Fell has argued that such homilies and letters from the Christian clergy and missionaries in Anglo-Saxon England, railing against 'polygamy' and 'incest', might well have been rhetorical, rather than an accurate representation of English behaviour.[10] She points out that the Anglo-Saxon penitentials – the codification of moral dogmas on which a harangue like this would be based – had been formulated beyond the shores of England, which suggests that they may have more properly reflected the conditions of their country of origin.[11] However, Patrick Wormald remarks that 'it is legitimate to wonder why they [the Anglo-Saxon penitentials] were then considered appropriate in England, and whether (or why) conditions in England were so very different from those of Italy, Gaul or Ireland'.[12]

We can see the influence of Christianity clearly in the laws of Aethelbert and Cnut. According to Aethelred, 'a Christian man ... shall never have more wives than one'.[13] Cnut echoes: 'he ... shall have no more wives than one and that shall be his wedded wife'. According to the *Law of the Northumbrian Priests* during the eleventh century, 'by virtue of God's prohibition, we forbid that any man should have more wives than one; and she is to be legally bequeathed and wedded'.[14]

It cannot be taken that all unions were in actual fact monogamous – there is always a distinction between legal theory and practice. Variation may also have existed between the Anglo-Saxon kingdoms. Nonetheless there is clear evidence of attempts to regulate marriage along monogamous lines.

The post-conquest period brought an emphasis on *publicly* regulated marriages. From 1280 onwards, for a marriage to be recognised as common law, banns had to be read out and a ceremony performed in church, and in the presence of a priest. But marriages which had not taken place in this manner were still recognised. The church preferred clandestine (but binding) marriages to concubinage and other unions that could be

dissolved at will.[15] Part of the reasoning behind the public insti-
tutionalisation of marriage was to try and ensure that impedi-
ments such as consanguinity could be brought out.[16]

For Chris Middleton, the emphasis on public regulation
represents

> not a battle within the ruling class, between Church and State,
> but a deliberate move to extend class control over an unregu-
> lated and recalcitrant peasantry. The fight was not between
> competing ecclesiastical and secular court systems but ... to
> ensure that serious matrimonial disputes came before a court
> at all – for the idea was deeply ingrained in the popular mind
> that marriage was a private contract, and not in need of public
> regulation.[17]

The connection between *class* interest and the regulation of marriage was explicitly stated by Thomas Cromwell in a ruling of 1538
which required all marriages to be recorded in parish registers.
Cromwell's stated intention was the 'avoiding of sundry strifes,
processes and contentions rising upon age, lineal descents, title of
inheritance, legitimation of bastardy . . .'.[18] During the eighteenth
century, as English society became increasingly commercialised,
Lord Hardwicke's Marriage Act (1753) made compulsory the
publication of banns, the purchase of a license, the presence of
two witnesses, and registration of the marriage. Falsification of the
register was made a capital offence.[19]

Considering the post-conquest period, then, it is not difficult
to tease out connections between sexual regulation and property
relations. Some forms of sexual regulation do indeed seem to
articulate the principle that *women themselves* were property.
Leywrite, for example, was a fine paid by a woman's father,
brother or lover or even the woman herself to her feudal lord in
cases of fornication.[20] It was intended to compensate the lord for
the loss of the merchet, which was a marriage fee paid by most
bondwomen (and some bondmen). As well as being a mark
of servility, it was intended to compensate lords for the loss of
chattels as well as the productive and reproductive capacities
of women.[21] Middleton argues that leywrite implied that women's
sexual worth was something that could be evaluated.

> Its functioning as a substitute for merchet depended on a recog-
> nition that peasant men valued virginity in their brides. It was

not the lord who was morally offended by a girl's fornication
(his losses could easily be recouped) but her potential suitors,
and consequently, her own father and family.[22]

However, Middleton considers that 'it does not follow that the
development of the peasantry's patriarchal morality was independent of the conditions of feudal production and class rule',[23] since

the sexual criteria by which peasant men judged potential wives
reflected essentially economic concerns ... the smooth transition of landed property, protection against uncontrolled
claims on the parental estate, and the desire to ensure that all
infants were pre-guaranteed material support.[24]

This was the case in Anglo-Saxon England too. A bridegroom
who was confident of his wife's virginity would have no worries
on any of these scores. The morning gift,[25] given to the bride the
morning after the consummation of the marriage, was essentially
an acknowledgement by the husband of her virginity. The law
codes of Alfred were also quite clearly concerned with the issue
of virginity:

If a young woman who is betrothed commits fornication she
shall pay compensation to the amount of 60 shillings to the
surety [of the marriage] if she is a commoner. This sum shall
be [paid] in livestock cattle being the property tendered, and
no slave shall be given such a payment. If her wergild is 60
shillings, she shall pay 100 shillings to the surety [of the mar-
riage]. If her wergild is 1200 shillings, she shall pay 120 shillings
to the surety.[26]

Such laws are indicative of a highly stratified class society. Not
only is the amount of compensation related to social class, pre-
marital chastity was one way of attempting to ensure the 'legitimacy' of heirs in the new propertied classes. Attempts to debar
widows from remarrying during the twelve-month 'mourning
period'[27] can similarly be explained as seeking to ensure that the
bride was not already pregnant, so that there would not be con-
flicting claims on her child and estate.

Aspects of law dealing with sexual assault demonstrate similar
values. Alfred decrees: 'If another man has previously lain with
her, then the compensation [for her violation] shall be half this
[amount]. If she is accused [of having] previously [lain with a

man], she shall clear herself [by an oath of] 60 hides, or lose half the compensation due her'.[28] This is an expression of the sexual double standard, a standard which derives from the fear of illegitimate children. Whether or not women have sexual relations with more than one partner is an issue in a class-based society, where the consideration of estates and the legitimacy of heirs is a prime consideration.

But this does not mean that practises such as polygamy and concubinage, where they existed in Anglo-Saxon society,[29] were antithetical to the maintenance of status. Vianna Muller sees polygamy as one way in which men who controlled surpluses used them to 'purchase' enhanced prestige in the shape of additional wives.[30] Jack Goody suggests that polygamy and concubinage could be used to provide a solution to childlessness,[31] providing an heir and the maintenance of status.[32] In this context he also points to conflicts between the church and other ruling groups: 'One possible reason for the suppression of secular concubinage... may have been its very ability to create "fictional" or additional heirs the existence of which might prevent a couple from donating its wealth for religious purposes'.[33]

The fact that the church's rulings in relation to monogamy actually received state sanction may (as in the case of divorce discussed below) indicate the way in which the Christian church could be used to bolster the mystique of kingship – monarch and church allied to their mutual benefit.

A consideration of the material interests of the Christian church may also help us to understand the regulation of marriage between kin. Unions between quite widely separated relatives were considered incestuous: modern limitations are much less strict.

The *Laws of the Northumbrian Priests* forbade marriage between persons within the fourth degree of kinship.[34] Aethelbert goes further: 'It must never happen that a Christian man marries within six degrees of relationship, that is within the fourth generation, or with the widow of a man as nearly related to him as this, or with a near relative of his first wife'.[35] Punishment for breaking such rules was heavy. Cnut ruled that 'if anyone commits incest, he shall make amends according to the degree of relationship either by the payment of wergild or of a fine, or by the forfeiture of all his possessions'.[36] Under Edward and Guthrum in the tenth century, 'in the case of incestuous unions, the councillors have decided that the King shall take possession of the male offender, before God and the world as the bishop shall prescribe, in accordance with the gravity of the offence'.[37]

Goody discusses how marriage between kin reinforces family ties and in the absence of sons can prevent property going outside the descent group, making less likely bequests which would enrich the church.[38] Whilst the church justified rulings against marriage between kin on moral grounds, on social grounds (the desirability of multiplying ties of kinship), and on physical grounds (the possibility of infertility),[39] Goody also observes that

> The encouragement of out marriage (exogamy) in a system that allocates property to women, especially as heiresses, would promote the dispersal of estates, and weaken the corporations of kin based upon them. At the very least such prohibitions enabled the church to exercise a large measure of control in the domestic domain, as was also the case when they took over the protection of widows and orphans. But they could also loosen the bonds of kinship and prevent the consolidation of estates where there were no male heirs.[40]

As the centuries advanced, it was made more and more difficult for couples, once married, to split up. During the Anglo-Saxon period, Aethelbert implies that divorce was allowed at the will of either one or both of the partners, with possible right of remarriage for both partners.

> If she wishes to depart with her children she shall have half the goods. If the husband wishes to keep [the children] she shall have a share of the goods equal to a child's. If she does not bear a child [her] father's relatives shall have her morning gift.[41]

One ground for divorce in early Anglo-Saxon England was a wife's infertility.[42] The prohibition of divorce might in such a case leave a family with no immediate male heirs.[43] But it was from just such a situation that the Christian church, eager to build up a landed endowment, stood to gain.[44]

As early as 673 we find the Synod of Hertford expressing the principle of the indissolubility of marriage, even though the spouses might have separated. Should a man 'put away the wife united to him in lawful wedlock, if he wish to be rightly a Christian, let him not be joined to another but remain as he is or else be reconciled to his wife'.[45] This was reaffirmed some three centuries later in the *Law of the Northumbrian Priests*. A layman was to 'lawfully keep a wife as long as she lives, unless... they both choose, with the Bishop's consent, to be separate and will henceforth observe chastity'.[46] According to George Howard, writing at the beginning of this century, 'from this time onwards, the indissolubility of marriage was imposed by the English Church under state sanction'.[47]

We have examined ways in which the regulation of sexual relationships in medieval England was motivated by property considerations. The question still remains, however, whether or not *women themselves* can correctly be viewed as property.

Societies which pre-date capitalism have been interpreted by anthropologists, historians and others as treating women as property – commodities. This perception, at first sight sympathetic to women, has itself been criticised by other scholars, feminist or otherwise, as androcentric, because it crudely oversimplifies the women's position, as well as often overlooking cultural or ritual observances. To perceive women simply as objects, denied 'subject status', is inadequate. They were not always slaves, they often had a political and a material existence in their own right, a degree of choice and some influence in decision taking; in all this they did have 'subject status'.

One compromise has been to argue that it is only *rights in* women which are commodified and exchanged. This approach allows women's subject status to remain intact because it nevertheless left them some areas of influence. Gerder Lerner for example argues that 'women never became "things", nor were they so perceived. Women... retained their power to act and to choose... But... their sexuality, an aspect of their body, was controlled by others....'[48] For Lerner 'it is not women who are reified and commodified, it is women's sexuality and reproductive capacity which is so treated'.[49]

It is certainly possible to describe situations in which women *were* active subjects in Anglo-Saxon England: queens, noble-women, abbesses and many upper-class women, for example, had access to not inconsiderable portions of property, providing them with a basis from which to exercise political power and authority. But this account still imposes the subject–object property nexus on to a situation in which it did not in historical fact exist.

The subject–object property nexus is specific to capitalism. It is only in capitalist society that property becomes an object, seemingly divorced from social relations. It is only in capitalist society that property is deemed to connote a disembodied characteristic inherent in the object. In capitalist society property has become a 'thing', a commodity which is freely disposable and which appears to bear no relationship to the structure of social relations. It is simply anachronistic to apply any such conception of property to English society until at least the sixteenth century. Another important feature of capitalist property relations is

> the legal separation of subject from subject in his or her capacity to have control over the disposal of a thing which has been designated his or her property . . . the separation of each person from his social relations and thus his social statuses such that each is related to the other as conceptually and legally equivalent.[50]

No such legal individuation existed in Anglo-Saxon England. For much of the Anglo-Saxon period, the kin group functioned as an organic collective, as we have already seen in our discussion of the rights and duties of kinship.

It is in these terms rather than in terms of purchase that we need to understand bride price. Marilyn Strathern's discussion of metaphoric and metonymic symbolisation is instructive in this context. Strathern points out that, whereas commodity exchange establishes a relation between the objects of a transaction, gift exchange establishes a relationship between subjects. Gift giving entails giving a part of oneself.[51]

In systems of metaphoric symbolisation, wealth or assets represent an aspect of intrinsic identity such as agnatic status or name. Disposal or withdrawal of them from the exchange system compromises identity. In metonymic symbolisation people exercise proprietorship over a second class of things – personal possessions, other valuables – in that they have personal rights of disposal. These 'things' are often regarded as products of the person's labour, creativity or energy. Although such things are disposable, making them *appear* like objects, unlike commodities they are not 'alienable'.

In an exchange a gift may metaphorically stand for the giver's 'name' or it may represent his or her labour metonymically. Superficially, items which are detachable (the disposable 'part' of a person as an identity) appear to be like 'objects' in metonymical exchange systems.[52] But this object-like appearance is deceptive. The relinquishing of these things, because they are part of a person, involves a loss. 'Compensation is paid to the person, not a price for the thing'.[53] In such situations there need not be the subject–object dichotomy characteristic of capitalist social relations. The system requires that items are replaced by others of equivalence taking their metonymical place, 'standing for the input of labour or creativity'.[54] Thus I would suggest that brideprice in Anglo-Saxon England is more instructively understood as a mechanism which marks the transference of rights in children and compensates the woman's family for her lost labour.

Women given or received in marriage can stand for aspects of collective identity which can be construed as purely male or both male and female.[55] We have seen that there was an agnatic/ patriarchal bias in Anglo-Saxon kinship and that there was a tendency towards virilocal residence patterns. But this did not mean that the system was patriarchal. It was rather an ego-centred bilateral one with descent and affiliation traced through both males and females, lacking any structural persistence across generations. Despite a male bias in the allocation of property, women were by no means excluded. (Further, whilst brideprice could be interpreted as emphasising the transferable parts of the collective identity as female, aspects of the system such as wergild do not present detachability as exclusively female.)

It is wrong, then, to construe brideprice as the purchase of women, who, as objects, are exchanged between groups of men as pieces of property. Similarly we should be wary of misinterpreting Alfred's law which states that:

A man may fight without becoming liable to a vendetta if he finds another [man] with his wedded wife, within closed doors or under the same blanket: or [if he finds another man] with his legitimate daughter [or sister]; or with his mother, if she has been given in lawful wedlock to his father.[56]

This does not signify that women were property: the rights and duties of kinship were such that an injury to one of its members would be an injury to the husband's community as a whole. Similarly, laws which award compensation to guardians or husbands in cases of adultery (e.g. Alfred's) cannot be interpreted in any simplistic way as evidence of proprietorial rights in women.

It has to be contextualised in terms of the workings of the kinship and legal system as a whole.

It is also questionable to interpret, as Basher does, laws relating to rape and abduction during the thirteenth, fourteenth and fifteenth centuries as being about 'the protection of male property in the form of their moveable goods, their wives and daughters, their bequeathed inheritances, their future heirs'.[57]

Placing rape and abduction side by side, as the laws of the time did, *did* inhibit the autonomy of women. But we have already seen that the freely-acting individual subject is not the legal concept of the person in feudal society. In feudal society a person was embedded in a set of social relations in a way that meant there was no concept of identical rights for all people regardless of their social status.[58] Pashukanis captures this well:

> All rights were considered as appertaining to a given concrete subject as limited group of subjects. Marx said that in the feudal world every right was a privilege. This epoch completely lacked any notion of a formal legal status common to all citizens.[59]

Basher observes that medieval rape laws were framed for the benefit of the wealthy and the protection of their property.[60] In a highly stratified society such as feudal England it is unsurprising that families would seek to protect their material interests. Rape or abduction of young women or men could be used as a strategy by the perpetrator to gain property and goods. And 'consenting rape' could be used by the partners as a plea to secure a liaison not approved by the woman's family.

Throughout much of the period covered in this book, choice of marital partner was subject to constraints right the way through the social structure.[61] It was usually men – fathers in particular – who were responsible for arranging marriages, and to that extent patriarchal relations were enshrined in the control of marriage. But we must not automatically assume that this set-up was, in intention, unconcerned with the interests of women. Restrictions on marriage choice can be seen as a way of ensuring that daughters did not marry too far 'down'. Jack Goody sees 'in' marriage as a method of preserving property and status.[62] 'Fathers try to arrange the marriage of their daughters to men of equal or superior standing'.[63]

We must also be wary of interpreting as a straightforward exercise of patriarchal power, the fact that full penalties for rape were not usually imposed (they could involve mutilation or castration). According to Basher, whilst male judges and juries were quite prepared to use the death penalty for crimes other than rape, they were 'loath to punish in any way other males for any sexual offence against females'.[64] Such a discrepancy between legal theory and practice may well be indicative of the institutionalised power of men. But such power cannot be separated from the whole structure and rationale of property relations in feudal England.

Throughout this chapter I have addressed the argument that women themselves have historically been considered property. That view is a simplistic one. It is clear that there was a general relationship between the regulation of sexual behaviour and property. But the perception that women *were* 'property' is actually symptomatic of a change in ways of thinking which only came about in the course of the transition from feudalism to capitalism. Ironically it enshrines a patriarchal ideology.

Conclusion

This book has been about the structural relationship between class and patriarchy, a relationship much debated but never satisfactorily resolved within the literature.

I have analysed class and patriarchy as interdependent factors within a single historical process. I have advanced the position that if social reality is perceived (as Marx in fact perceived it) as a complex network of *internal relations* within which any single element is what it is only by virtue of its relation to others – a dialectical rather than an atomistic perception of social reality – then the question as to which of the two axes of social division has primacy is revealed as a misplaced one.

Just as the concepts of labour and capital contain each other – neither category can be defined without reference to the other – so, for the period of English history addressed in this study, do the categories of class and patriarchy contain each other. It is my argument that class and patriarchy have been *organically* rather than accidentally or contingently related. Because class and patriarchy have been organically connected we cannot draw hard-and-fast boundaries around them. The relationship between them has been a symbiotic one.

We have been able to identify patriarchal relations in Anglo-Saxon society, and feudal and capitalist England. Indeed each of those societies has been constructed *through* patriarchal relations. The principle and practice of primogeniture, which had begun to emerge in the Anglo-Saxon period and remained the law of England until 1925,[1] is a key example of this. Primogeniture enforced male domination, and facilitated the consolidation of property crucial to class power. In England class relations cannot be understood without reference to patriarchy. Anglo-Saxon, feudal and capitalist society in England would not have taken the *forms* that they did if patriarchal social relations had been absent. That is not to say that barbarian, feudal or capitalist society in England could not have been constructed without patriarchal relations. My argument is that an understanding of those societies in England demands an understanding of patriarchal relations. It is possible that barbarian, feudal and capitalist society *could* have been constructed *without* patriarchal relations. But in England they were *not*. Patriarchal relations have been an integral part of each of those societies. Nor can we understand patriarchy without reference to different historical forms of property and class relations in England. The degree and intensity of patriarchal relations in England has varied according to social rank.

What I have argued is not incompatible with the view advanced in recent years by socialist feminists that class relations are patriarchal and that patriarchal relations are classed.[2] However, that position has never been developed from within an internal relations perspective. An internal relations perspective on the nature of class and patriarchy enables us to see that terms such as primacy and autonomy have been misplaced. They can only be properly grasped as misplaced once we begin to analyse class and patriarchy as symbiotic parts of a single process.

Like Marx I see property as a key axis upon which social divisions turn, and it is through an analysis of property that we can develop a unified systems analysis of class and patriarchy. If we place property relations at the heart of an analysis of social divisions as constructed by, as expressions of and actually in turn constitutive of, patriarchal relations, we can see that questions regarding the primacy of particular divisions are not appropriate.

Class relations are constructed and exist in and through property relations. But property relations can exist without class relations – tribal structures are a case in point. Anthropologists and historians demonstrate that patriarchy has often been associated with non-classed property relations. That does not mean, though, that all forms of property relations historically have involved patriarchal relations. But it is certainly demonstrable that patriarchal relations existed in pre-capitalist England. It is also demonstrable that patriarchy has existed in England coincidentally with capitalist property forms. Both class and patriarchy are shown in this study to be particular expressions of the fundamental social relation of property, which they together constitute.[3]

It may be objected that such a solution to the structural debate about class and patriarchy reifies the category of property, and is economistic. Ironically, however, that sort of criticism is itself symptomatic of the fetishes of the capitalist mode of production. Capitalism separates economic, political and kinship structures from one another. That separation permits a narrow equation between property relations and relations of production, defined as 'the economy', which in turn is more often than not defined at the level of the labour process. A solution to the structural debate about class and patriarchy which hinges on property relations can only be accused of reification if property is narrowly equated with the economy.

Attention to the historical and empirical data reveals such an equation to be fundamentally mistaken. We cannot understand property relations in pre-capitalist England without reference to kinship and political structures. In Anglo-Saxon society, for example, kingship, a social relation intimately bound up with property, evolved in many instances through the development of hierarchical leadership structures within extended families.[4] Some of Marx's observations on feudal society are also instructive. Because the direct producer was in possession of the means of production, 'the property relationship ... appear[ed] as a direct relationship of lordship and servitude'.[5] Relations of personal dependence were essential to feudal property forms. And '*feudalism* ... was *directly political*, that is to say, the elements of civil life, for example, property, or the family, or the mode of labour, were raised to the level of political life in the form of seigniority, estates and corporations'.[6]

Nor can we properly separate out superstructural elements from property relations in capitalist England. Political and legal structures – e.g. enclosure acts, laws regulating hours of work and rates of pay, etc. – have defined property relations. Although the family is outside of the direct point of production, inheritance strategies within families have remained essential to the consolidation and furtherance of class power.

If class and patriarchy are both constitutive of and expressions of changing forms of property relations, then questions about the nature and degree of patriarchal *autonomy* can also be seen as inappropriate. I have demonstrated that we cannot separate class relations and patriarchal relations in English history in any meaningful way: they were mutually reinforcing. There is of course no a priori reason to assume that class relations cannot exist in a non-patriarchal form or that patriarchal relations necessarily have to entail class relations. But as far as England is concerned, during the period under consideration, class and patriarchy were inextricably linked. We cannot really talk about patriarchal autonomy in a structural sense.

Theories about the autonomy of patriarchy were of course advanced partly in an attempt to avoid reductionism, a characteristic trait of certain variants of Marxism. It is ironical, then, that claims for the autonomy of patriarchy are themselves reductionist.

Theories about the autonomy of patriarchy also surfaced against the backdrop of the rise of structural Marxism, which assumed that the economy is separate from other levels of the social structure. E. P. Thompson was one of the fiercest critics of such academic fiction.[7] A quote from his brilliant polemic against Althusser is apposite here. I have taken the liberty of substituting the term patriarchy where Thompson refers to law.

> I have, as it happens, been interested in this myself, in my historical practice: not, of course, in any grand way – for the whole of history, nor for the capitalist mode of production everywhere, but in a very petty conjuncture: in an island on the edge of the Atlantic. So my evidence is highly marginal, as well as being seriously contaminated by empirical content . . . I found that patriarchy did not keep politely to a 'level' but was at every bloody level; it was imbricated within the mode of production and productive relations themselves (as property-rights, definitions of agrarian practice) and it was simultaneously present in the philosophy of Locke . . . reappearing bewigged and gowned in the guise of ideology; it danced a cotillion with religion . . . it was an arm of politics and politics was one of its arms . . . it contributed to the definition of the self-identity, both of rulers and ruled. . . .[8]

All of this does not prevent us recognising that men have often pursued their own interests (or assumed interests) against women's. My discussion of demands for a family wage, and of the explicit exclusion of women from the franchise for example, assumes this as part of the explanation. Indeed, in many ways the individualisation of capitalist property relations gives greater scope for the distinct articulation of social divisions between women and men. This in turn can foster the impression that

patriarchy can be defined in itself as an autonomous entity, ultimately independent from other social divisions, i.e. an *external
entity, interacting* with, in this case, the class division. Just as it
appears that 'superstructures' are separate from the 'base', it may
also appear that patriarchy is ultimately separate from other
social divisions. But this is a piece of idealist fiction produced by
the material conditions of capitalist society.

Throughout this book I have also been addressing a longstanding lacuna within historical sociology: the role of patriarchy in
the transition from feudalism to capitalism. The controversy on
the transition from feudalism to capitalism, regarded as one of the
most important historical debates in recent years, has covered a
range of opinions. My focus was upon contributions from within
the Marxist tradition, in particular the 'internal property relations
perspective'. The 'history men' who advanced those contributions
never considered the extent to which patriarchy affected or was
affected by the transition from feudalism to capitalism.

I have not myself attempted to develop a feminist analysis of
the specific and detailed issues raised by those authors. It is a
task which requires further research. I have nonetheless been
addressing the role of patriarchy in the transition from feudalism
to capitalism. I have done so from within a Marxist property
relations perspective. I have shown that in England patriarchal
relations both contributed to and were changed by the transition
from feudalism to capitalism.

At the heart of the transition was a fundamental shift in property relations. In England that shift was accomplished through
property relations which were patriarchally structured. Inheritance through the male line facilitated the accumulation of property central to the maintenance and consolidation of class power
in feudal society. It did so in 'economic' terms. It did so too in
'political' terms. The patriarchal structuring of the feudal polity
was an inevitable consequence of the symbiotic relationship
between property and political structures in feudal England.
Whereas in Anglo-Saxon society I argued that the position of
women within kinship structures was contradictory – they might
be equal 'sisters' but subordinate daughters and wives – I characterised the position of women within the family in feudal England
and with the emergence of capitalism as subordinate daughters
and wives. However, I refuted the view that women, either in
Anglo-Saxon society or feudal England were themselves property.

The view that women were property is actually founded upon a change in ways of thinking about property which came about with the development of property forms specific to capitalism. That view also enshrines a patriarchal ideology.

Property forms specific to capitalism developed in and through property relations in feudal society that were patriarchally structured. Capitalist forms of property too have been patriarchally structured. Feudal property was transformed into modern individualistic ownership. Property became a right to objects or commodities, material *things*. In capitalist society property involves rights of legal individuals to exclude others. Given the long historical patriarchal structuring of property relations, the effects of which permeated right the way through the social structure, it is unsurprising that the individualistic nature of capitalist property relations has often involved the assertion of the rights of men over those of women. This patriarchal division has been articulated in, for example, the ideology of the male breadwinner. It has also been articulated in the political sphere. Because of the preference for male heirs in feudal society women were usually, de facto, excluded from the polity – 'the law of the father'. With the development of capitalism women were *explicitly* excluded from citizenship – the 'capitalist fraternity'. Both the ideology of the male breadwinner and women's exclusion from citizenship added weight to the subordination of women as daughters and wives.

However, the individualistic nature of capitalist property relations has created contradictions in patriarchal relations. It has thrown up the ideological possibility and reality of women as individual property owners, and of women as citizens. It has also provided a platform from which women can challenge their subordinate status as daughters and wives. It is a contradiction of course which has been seized upon by feminists. However, feminism is ultimately limited in vision and impact where it does not also challenge the reality of capitalist social relations as a major axis of stratification and domination and subordination, which, if maintained, will preclude the possibility of true equality for all individuals regardless of sex or gender.

Notes

INTRODUCTION

1 M. Barrett, *Women's Oppression Today* (second edition), London, Verso, 1988, p. xxxiv.

2 J. F. Lyotard, *The Post Modern Condition: A Report on Knowledge*, Manchester, Manchester University Press, 1984 (English translation).

3 Postmodern feminism and critiques of it can be followed up through L. Nicholson, (ed.) *Feminism/Postfeminism*, London, Routledge, 1990; J. Flax, *Thinking Fragments*, Berkeley and Los Angeles, University of California Press, 1990; P. Waugh, *Feminine Fictions*, London, Routledge, 1989; 'From Modernism, Postmodernism, Feminism: Gender and Autonomy Theory', in P. Waugh (ed.), *Postmodernism*, London, Edward Arnold, 1992.

4 F. Jameson, 'Postmodernism, or the Cultural Logic of Late Capitalism', *New Left Review*, 146, 1984, pp. 53–92; see also 'The Politics of Theory: Ideological Positions in the Post-Modern Debate', *New German Critique*, 33, 1984, pp. 53–65.

5 D. Harvey, *The Condition of Postmodernity*, Oxford, Basil Blackwell, 1989.

6 Ibid. e.g. p. 51.

7 A. Callinicos, *Against Postmodernism*, Cambridge, Polity Press, 1989, pp. 168–171.

8 K. Marx, *Capital*, Vol. 1, Middlesex, Pelican, 1976, Chapters 26–30.

9 M. Weber, *The Protestant Ethic and the Spirit of Capitalism*, London, Allen and Unwin, 1930.

10 The transition debate can be followed up through R. Brenner, 'Agrarian Class Structure and Economic Development in Pre-industrial Europe', *Past and Present*, 70, 1976; 'The Origins of Capitalist Development: A Critique of Neo-Smithian Marxism', *New Left Review*, 104, 1977; 'Agrarian Class Structure and Economic Development in Preindustrial Europe', *Past and Present*, 97, 1982; M. Dobb, (1946), *Studies in the Development of Capitalism*, London, Routledge & Kegan Paul, 1963 reprint; M. Postan, 'Some Economic Evidence of Declining Population in the late Middle Ages', Economic History

Review, 3, 1950; 'England', in M. Postan (ed.), *Cambridge Economic History of Europe*, Vol. I, Cambridge, Cambridge University Press; *Essays on Medieval Agriculture*, Cambridge, Cambridge University Press, 1973; P. Sweezey, 'The Transition from Feudalism to Capitalism', *Science and Society*, 14, 1950; I. Wallerstein, *The Modern World System*, New York, Academic Press, 1974; 'From Feudalism to Capitalism', *Social Forces*, 55, 1976; *The Modern World System*, II, New York, Academic Press, 1980; Hilton, R. (ed.), *The Transition from Feudalism to Capitalism*, London, Verso, 1978; T. H. Aston and C. H. E. Philpin (eds), *The Brenner Debate*, Cambridge, Cambridge University Press, 1987; R. J. Holton, *The Transition from Feudalism to Capitalism*, London, Macmillan, 1985.

1 THE DEBATE

1 F. Engels (1884), 'The Origins of the Family, Private Property and the State', in K. Marx and F. Engels, *Selected Works*, London, Lawrence and Wishart, 1968, p. 488.
2 K. Marx and F. Engels (1848), 'The Communist Manifesto', in D. McLennan (ed.), *Karl Marx: Selected Writings*, Oxford, Oxford University Press, 1977, p. 227.
3 Ibid.
4 K. Millet, *Sexual Politics*, London, Sphere, 1971, pp. 24–25.
5 S. Firestone, *The Dialectic of Sex*, London, The Women's Press, 1979; see Rosalind Delmar's Introduction, e.g. pp. 8–9.
6 H. Hartmann, *The Unhappy Marriage of Marxism and Feminism*, London, Pluto Press, 1981, p. 14.
7 Ibid., p. 15.
8 C. Delphy (translated D. Leonard), 'The Main Enemy', in *Close to Home*, London, Hutchinson, 1984, pp. 57–77.
9 S. Walby, *Theorizing Patriarchy*, Oxford, Basil Blackwell, 1990, p. 20.
10 R. McDonough, and R. Harrison, 'Patriarchy and Relations of Production', in A. Kuhn and A. M. Wolpe (eds), *Feminism and Materialism*, London, Routledge & Kegan Paul, 1980, p. 40.
11 Z. Eisenstein, *Capitalist Patriarchy and the Case for Socialist Feminism*, New York, Monthly Review Press, 1979, p. 22.
12 J. Mitchell, *Psychoanalysis and Feminism*, Middlesex, Penguin, 1975, p.xvi.
13 M. Barrett, *Women's Oppression Today*, London, Verso, 1988, p.xiii.
14 Ibid.
15 Engels (1884) in Marx and Engels, op. cit., 1968, p. 495.
16 McDonough and Harrison, op. cit., p. 25.
17 Eisenstein, op. cit., p. 2.
18 Ibid., p. 25.
19 Mitchell, op. cit., passim.
20 Millet, op. cit., p. 29.
21 Ibid., p. 31.
22 Ibid., p. 29.

23 Firestone, op. cit., p. 12.
24 Ibid., p. 20.
25 Ibid., p. 17.
26 Hartmann, op. cit., p. 16.
27 Ibid., pp. 15–16.
28 Delphy, op. cit.
29 Walby, op. cit., p. 21.
30 Quoted in D. Binns, 'Marx and Engels on the Family: Production and Reproduction in Historical Materialism,' unpublished paper, University of Glasgow, 1983, p. 15.
31 Quoted in L. Colletti, *Early Writings*, Middlesex, Penguin, 1975, p. 22.
32 Ibid., p. 20.
33 Mitchell, op. cit., p. 37.
34 Ibid., p. 37.
35 K. Marx (1845), 'Theses on Feuerbach', in McLellan, op. cit., pp. 156–157.
36 K. Marx (1846), 'The German Ideology', in ibid., pp. 164–165.
37 K. Marx (1867), *Capital*, Vol. I, Middlesex, Penguin, 1976. See discussions in Mandell's introduction, pp. 38–54 and Chapters 1, 26 and 27.
38 G. Lerner, *The Creation of Patriarchy*, Oxford, Oxford University Press, 1986, p. 52.
39 Ibid., p. 40.
40 Ibid., pp. 41–42.
41 Ibid., p. 44.
42 Ibid., p. 42.
43 See for example Lerner's discussion (op. cit.) of C. Meillasoux and P. Aaby. Meillasoux in 'From Reproduction to Production', in *Economy and Society*, 1(1), 1972, suggests that the acquisition of private property was preceded by control over reproduction. P. Aaby, 'Engels and Women', in *Critique of Anthropology*, 3 (9/10), attempts to turn Engels on his head, arguing that the appropriation of the labour of women as reproducers was the first appropriation of private property.
44 M. Molyneux, 'Beyond the Domestic Labour Debate', *New Left Review*, 116, 1979, p. 14.
45 Ibid., p. 16.
46 K. Marx (1859), 'Preface to a Critique of Political Economy', in McLellan, op. cit., p. 389.
47 Ibid., p. 390.
48 One of the problems with the base–superstructure model is that of substituting economism for historical materialism. Marx's use of the base–superstructure metaphor in 'The German Ideology' can be seen as *polemical* in intent – i.e. directed against idealist philosophy.
49 K. Marx (1857/8), *Grundrisse*, Middlesex, Penguin, 1973, p. 472.
50 K. Marx (1894), *Capital*, Vol. III, London, Lawrence & Wishart, 1974, p. 790.
51 Some of the vast literature on the state and class society includes

K. Marx (1852), 'The Eighteenth Brumaire of Louis Bonaparte', in Marx and Engels, 1968, op. cit; V. Lenin, (1918) 'The State and Revolution', in *Lenin: Collected Works*, Moscow, Progress, 1977; A. Gramsci, 'State and Civil Society', in *Selection from the Prison Notebooks*, London, Lawrence & Wishart, 1971; R. Miliband, *The State in Capitalist Society*, London, Quartet, 1973.

52 As similarly noted in relation to Delphy by M. Barrett and M. McIntosh, 'Christine Delphy: Towards a Materialist Feminism?' *Feminist Review*, 1, 1979.

53 In arguing that the oppression common to all women is the appropriation common to all women, most of her evidence relates to rural non-industrial households. See Barrett and McIntosh, ibid., p. 97 for an elaboration of this point.

54 Ibid., pp. 102–103 for a discussion of similar points.

55 S. Walby, *Patriarchy at Work*, Cambridge, Polity, 1986, pp. 52- 54 for points discussed here.

56 Mitchell, 1975, op. cit., p. 412.

57 Ibid., p. 410.

58 The arguments in J. Mitchell, *Women's Estate*, Middlesex, Penguin, 1971, derive from Althusser's 'Contradiction and Overdetermination' as well as 'On the Materialist Dialectic', in L. Althusser, *For Marx*, London, Allen Lane, 1970.

59 Mitchell, 1971, op. cit., p. 101.

60 Mitchell, 1975, op. cit., p. 406 and quoted in McDonough and Harrison, op. cit., p. 22.

61 Mitchell, 1975, op. cit., and quoted in McDonough and Harrison, op. cit., p. 23.

62 McDonough and Harrison, op. cit., p. 28, and quoted in V. Beechey, op. cit., p. 77.

63 Eisenstein, op. cit., p. 1.

64 Quoted in Firestone, op. cit., p. 13.

65 Ibid., p. 14.

66 Ibid., p. 18.

67 Ibid., p. 14.

68 Ibid., pp. 20–21.

69 Ibid., p. 20.

70 Ibid., p. 19.

71 Millet, op. cit., p. 25.

72 Ibid., p. 33.

73 Ibid., p. 38.

74 Ibid.

75 Ibid.

76 Ibid., p. 36.

77 Hartmann, op. cit., p. 19.

78 Ibid., p. 29.

79 Ibid., pp. 27–28.

80 Ibid., p. 24.

81 Ibid.

82 Ibid., p. 30.

83 Ibid., p. 32.
84 Ibid., p. 17.
85 Ibid., p. 26.
86 Ibid., p. 30.
87 Delphy, op. cit.
88 Walby, 1990, op. cit., p. 200.
89 See R. Keat and J. Urry, *Social Theory as Science*, London, Rout-ledge & Kegan Paul (second edition), 1982, for a discussion of models of causation in the social sciences; also, T. Benton, *Philosophical Foundations of the Three Sociologies*, London, Routledge & Kegan Paul, 1977 and Ollman, *Alienation* (second edition), Cambridge, Cambridge University Press, 1976.
90 McDonough and Harrison, op. cit., p. 24.
91 This criticism of Mitchell draws on a critique of Althusser by S. Clarke, 'Althusserian Marxism', in S. Clarke, T. Lovell, K. McDonnell, K. Robins and V. Jeleniewski-Seidler (eds), *One-Dimensional Marxism*, London, Allison & Busby, 1980, pp. 6–102.
92 As noted by Beechey, op. cit., pp. 76–77.
93 Ibid., p. 77.
94 See discussion of Max Weber's 'Ideal Types', in A. Giddens, *Capitalism and Modern Social Theory*, London, Cambridge University Press, 1971, pp. 141–143.
95 Hartmann, op. cit., pp. 17, 30.
96 Walby, 1990, op. cit., p. 20.
97 Ibid., p. 20.
98 Molyneux, op. cit., p. 15.
99 Ibid., p. 15 and Delphy, op. cit., p. 74.
100 Molyneux, op. cit., p. 15.
101 Ibid., p. 17.
102 Walby, 1990, op. cit., p. 177.
103 Ibid., p. 200.

2 A WAY FORWARD

1 For a discussion of this see D. Sayer, *The Violence of Abstraction*, Oxford, Basil Blackwell, 1987, Chapter 2; Sayer's discussion of internal relations draws on the work of B. Ollman, *Alienation* (second edition), Cambridge, Cambridge University Press, 1976.
2 For a discussion and critique of the Marxism of the Second International (a body that sought to coordinate various socialist parties in the quarter century preceding the First World War) see L. Colletti, *From Rousseau to Lenin*, London, New Left Books, 1972.
3 K. Marx, 'Preface to a contribution to the critique of Political Economy', in Marx and Engels *Selected Works*, London, Lawrence & Wishart, 1968, pp. 181–182.
4 See L. Althusser, 'Contradiction and Overdetermination' and 'On the Materialist Dialectic', in *For Marx*, London, Allen Hare, 1970.
5 See Sayer op. cit., e.g. p. 20.

6 K. Marx, *Grundrisse*, Middlesex, Penguin, 1973, General Introduction, p. 101, and quoted in Sayer op. cit., p. 20.
7 Marx, *Grundrisse*, op. cit., p. 88 and quoted in Sayer op. cit., p. 20.
8 Marx, ibid., Sayer, ibid.
9 Marx, ibid., p. 472.
10 K. Marx, *Capital*, Vol. III, London, Lawrence & Wishart, 1974, p. 790.
11 See e.g. R. Miliband, *The State in Capitalist Society*, London, Quartet, 1973; M. MacIntosh, 'The State and the Oppression of Women', in A. Kuhn, and A. M. Wolpe (eds), *Feminism and Materialism*, London, Routledge & Kegan Paul, 1980.
12 Quoted in Sayer, op. cit., p. 62.
13 Kate Millet, *Sexual Politics*, London, Sphere, 1971, p. 25.
14 S. Firestone, *The Dialectic of Sex*, London, The Women's Press, 1979, p. 75.
15 H. Hartmann, *The Unhappy Marriage of Marxism and Feminism*, London, Pluto Press, 1981, pp. 15 and 25.
16 R. McDonough and R. Harrison, 'Patriarchy and Relations of Production', in A. Kuhn and A. M. Wolpe (eds), *Feminism and Materialism*, Routledge & Kegan Paul, London, 1980, p. 40.
17 Z. Eisenstein, *Capitalist Patriarchy and the Case for Socialist Feminism*, New York, Monthly Review Press, 1979, p. 20.
18 J. Mitchell, *Psychoanalysis and Feminism*, Middlesex, Penguin, 1975, p. 377.
19 S. Walby, *Theorizing Patriarchy*, Oxford, Basil Blackwell, 1990, p. 200.
20 Ibid.
21 R. Hilton, *Bond Men Made Free*, London, Methuen, 1977, p. 14.
22 V. Muller, 'The Formation of the State and the Oppression of Women: Some Theoretical Considerations and a Case Study in England and Wales', *Review of Radical Political Economy*, 9, 1977, pp. 13, 15, 16.
23 Ibid., p. 8; E. A. Thomson, *The Early Germans*, Oxford, Oxford University Press, 1966, Chapters 1 and 2. See also P. Anderson, *Passages from Antiquity to Feudalism*, London, Verso, 1974, pp. 107–111.
24 Anderson, 1974, op. cit., p. 158.
25 Ibid., p. 159.
26 Ibid., p. 123.
27 T. M. Charles Edwards, 'Kinship, Status and the Origins of the Hide', *Past and Present*, 56, 1972, pp. 7–14.
28 D. Whitelock, *The Beginnings of English Society*, Harmondsworth, Penguin, 1952, p. 98; see also pp. 99–102 for a discussion of the various classes who held land from a lord.
29 Edwards, op. cit., p. 35.
30 Ibid., p. 18.
31 Anderson, op. cit., p. 124.
32 Ibid., p. 159.
33 Muller, op. cit., p. 15.

34 Anderson, op. cit., p. 159.
35 Ibid., p. 124.
36 Ibid., p. 158.
37 Hobsbawm in R. Hilton (ed.), *The Transition from Feudalism to Capitalism*, London, Verso, 1978, p. 161.
38 Anderson, op. cit., p. 158.
39 Ibid., pp. 160–161.
40 Hobsbawm in Hilton, 1978, op. cit., p. 161.
41 Ibid.
42 See Hilton, 1978, op cit., 'A Note on Feudalism', p. 30.
43 Useful sources include Hilton, 1977, op. cit., Chapter 1; M. Bloch, *Feudal Society*, Vol. 1, part V, London, Routledge & Kegan Paul, 1962; Anderson, op. cit., pp. 147–153; Hilton, 1978, op. cit., Introduction.
44 Hilton, 1978, op. cit., pp. 25–26.
45 Ibid., p. 17.
46 Hobsbawm in Hilton, 1978, op. cit., pp. 161–162, and see K. Marx, *Capital*, Vol. I, part 8, London, Penguin, 1976.
47 Quoted in Hilton, 1978, op. cit., p. 145.
48 Quoted in ibid., p. 146.
49 M. Weber, *The Protestant Ethic and the Spirit of Capitalism*, London: Allen & Unwin, 1930.
50 See e.g. K. Marx, 'Wage Labour and Capital', in D. McLellan, *Karl Marx: Selected Writings*, Oxford, Oxford University Press, 1977, pp. 248–268.

3 MARXISM AND THE TRANSITION FROM FEUDALISM TO CAPITALISM

1 For Marx's explanation of the transition from feudalism to capitalism see *Capital*, Vol. I, London, Penguin, 1976, Chapters 26–32.
2 Ibid., Chapter 28.
3 Ibid., p. 889
4 P. Sweezey 'The Transition from Feudalism to Capitalism', *Science and Society*, 14, 1950.
5 I. Wallerstein, *The Modern World System*, New York, Academic Press, 1974; 'From Feudalism to Capitalism', *Social Forces*, 55, 1976; *The Modern World System*, New York, Academic Press, 1980.
6 Wallerstein, 1974, op. cit., p. 401.
7 R. Brenner, 'The Origins of Capitalist Development: A Critique of Neo-Smithian Marxism', *New Left Review*, 104, 1977.
8 S. Clarke, 'Socialist Humanism and the Critique of Economism', *History Workshop*, 8, 1979.
9 M. Dobb, *Studies in the Development of Capitalism*, London, Routledge & Kegan Paul, 1963; J. Merrington, 'Town and Country in the Transition to Capitalism', *New Left Review*, 93, 1975.
10 P. Bairoch, 'Geographical Structure and Trade Balance of Foreign Trade', *Journal of European Economic History*, 3, 1974; P. O'Brien,

'European Economic Development: The Contribution of the Periphery', *Economic History Review*, 35(1), 1982.

11 K. Marx, *Capital*, Vol. III, London, Lawrence and Wishart, 1974, p. 327.

12 Dobb, 1963, op. cit., 'Reply', *Science and Society*, 14, 1950.

13 R. Hilton, (ed.), *The Decline of Serfdom in Medieval England*, London, Macmillan, 1969; *Bond Men Made Free, Medieval Peasant Movements and the English Rising of 1381*, London, Methuen, 1977; 'Introduction' in R. Hilton (ed.), *The Transition from Feudalism to Capitalism*, London, Verso, 1978.

14 R. J. Holton, *The Transition from Feudalism to Capitalism*, London, Macmillan, 1985, p. 82.

15 R. Brenner, 'Agrarian Class Structure and Economic Development in Pre-industrial Europe', *Past and Present*, 70, 1976.

16 Ibid., p. 31.

17 See M. Postan, *The Medieval Economy and Society*, Harmondworth, Pelican, 1975; 'Some Economic Evidence of Declining Population in the late Middle Ages', *Economic History Review*, 3, 1950; 'England', in M. Postan (ed.), *Cambridge Economic History of Europe*, Vol. I, Cambridge, Cambridge University Press, 1966; *Essays on Medieval Agriculture*, Cambridge, Cambridge University Press, 1973.

18 R. Brenner, 'Agrarian Class Structure and Economic Development in Pre-industrial Europe', *Past and Present*, 97, 1982.

19 K. Marx, *The Poverty of Philosophy*, New York International, 1973, p. 154 and quoted in D. Sayer, *The Violence of Abstraction*, Oxford, Basil Blackwell, 1987, p. 21.

20 Sayer, op. cit., p. 60.

21 M. Bloch, *Feudal Society*, Vol. I, London, Routledge & Kegan Paul, 1965, pp. 115–116.

22 K. Marx, *Capital*, Vol. III, op. cit., p. 790.

23 S. F. C. Milson, *Historical Foundations of the Common Law*, London, Butterworths, 1969, p. 332, as discussed in A. Reeve, *Property*, London, Macmillan, 1986, p. 49.

24 W. S. Holdsworth, *A History of English Law* (second edition), Vol. 7, London, Sweet and Maxwell, 1937, p. 458 and quoted in Reeve, op. cit., p. 49.

25 G. Aylmer, 'The Meaning and Definition of "Property" in Seventeenth-Century England,' *Past and Present*, 86, 1980, pp. 87–97. This is also noted by Reeve, op. cit., p. 49.

26 C. B. Macpherson, *Democratic Theory*, Oxford, Clarendon Press, 1973, p. 122.

27 Ibid.

28 Quoted in Sayer, op. cit., p. 63.

29 Quoted in ibid.

30 For a general if somewhat technical discussion of rights and duties associated with ownership see Reeve, op. cit., Chapter 2.

31 K. Marx, 1880, 'Marginal Notes on A. Wagner, Lehrbuch der Politis-

chen Okonomie', *Theoretical Practice*, 5, 1972, p. 210 and quoted in Sayer op. cit., p. 55.
32 Much of my analysis in the following chapters has been developed from looking at law. In doing this I have made certain methodological assumptions. I have assumed that law reflects social conditions, i.e. that law arises from conditions and situations it seeks to guide and control. I have also assumed that laws are made when a practice exists and that those practices are seen as a problem. For example: if everyone or no-one has sexual relations outside marriage then law is not necessary to allow or attempt to prevent sex outside marriage. But laws against adultery and polygamy, for example, would indicate that such relations exist and that they are seen as problematic in a particular society.

I am also aware that what the law prescribes is not necessarily practised, that a disjuncture between legal theory and practice can exist. Nor does law tell us about the actuality of peoples lives; it is also often developed and imposed by dominant classes.

We should then be wary about too literal an interpretation of law. However, law *does* offer us rough guidelines about the social structures from which they derive. Laws tell us what was deemed to be acceptable and unacceptable. Thus, at the very least laws can tell us about the values of a society.
33 Where law is used as a source for historical analysis of Anglo-Saxon society we cannot assume that laws which existed in one kingdom necessarily existed in all kingdoms. We should therefore also be cautious about how we interpret chronological change.

4 PROPERTY AND PATRIARCHY

1 J. McNamara and S. Wemple, 'Sanctity and Power: The Dual Pursuit of Medieval Women', in R. Bridenthal and C. Koonz (eds) *Becoming Visible: Women in European History*, Boston, Houghton Mifflin, 1977, p. 104.
2 C. Fell, *Women in Anglo-Saxon England*, Bloomington, Indiana State University Press, 1984, pp. 89–90.
3 Ibid., p. 4.
4 V. Muller, 'The Formation of the State and the Oppression of Women: Some Theoretical Considerations and a Case Study in England and Wales', *Review of Radical Political Economy*, 9, 1977, p. 18.
5 Ibid., p. 16.
6 M. Meyer, 'Land Charters and the Legal Position of Anglo-Saxon Women', in B. Kanner (ed.), *The Women of England from Anglo-Saxon Times to the Present: Interpretative Bibliographical Essays*, London, Mansell, 1980, p. 61 and Muller, op. cit., pp. 15–16.
7 P. Wormald, *Bede and The Conversion of England: The Charter Evidence* (Jarrow Lecture, 1984), [Jarrow] [St Paul's Church, 1985], pp. 20–23 and personal communication, 1989.

8 F. Pollock and W. Maitland, *History of English Law Before the Time of Edward I*, Vol. I, Cambridge, Cambridge University Press, 1898, pp. 62- 63.

9 Ibid., p. 60.

10 T. M. Charles Edwards, 'Kinship, Status and the Origins of the Hide', *Past and Present*, 56, 1972, pp. 7–14; D. Whitelock, *The Beginnings of English Society*, Harmondsworth, Penguin, 1952, p. 98; see also pp. 99–102, for a discussion of the various classes who held land from lords.

11 Meyer, op. cit., p. 70.

12 Ibid., pp. 59–61.

13 Ibid., p. 64.

14 C. Edwards, 'The Distinction Between Land and Moveable Wealth in Anglo-Saxon England', in P. H. Sawyer (ed.), *English Medieval Settlement*, London, Edward Arnold, 1979, pp. 100–101; D. H. Farmer (ed.) *The Age of Bede*, Harmondsworth, Penguin Classics; Fell, op. cit., pp. 89–90.

15 D. Whitelock (ed.), *English Historical Documents*, London, Methuen, 1979, law 38, p. 403.

16 A. L. Klinck, 'Anglo-Saxon Women and the Law', *Journal of Medieval History*, 8, 1982, p. 113.

17 Pollock and Maitland, Vol. II, op. cit., pp. 263–264.

18 Wormald, personal communication, 1989, op. cit.; see J. C. Holt, 'The Origins of the Constitutional Tradition in England', in *Magna Carta and Medieval Government*, London, Hambledon Press, 1985, pp. 9–11 for discussion on the Kentish submission and custom.

19 See, for example, J. C. Holt, 'Feudal Society and the Family in Early Medieval England: The Heiress and the Alien', *Transactions of the Royal Historical Society*, 35, 1985.

20 J. C. Holt, 'Politics and Property in Early Medieval England', *Past and Present*, 57, 1972, p. 42.

21 J. Thirsk, 'The Common Fields', *Past and Present*, 29, 1964, pp. 12–13.

22 G. D. G. Hall (trans), *The Treatise on the Laws and Customs of the Realm of England Commonly Called Glanville*, Oxford, Oxford University Press, 1965, p. 75.

23 S. E. Thorne (trans), *Bracton on the Laws and Customs of England*, Vol. II, Cambridge, MA: Harvard University Press, 1968, p. 190.

24 Ibid., p. 188.

25 J. Thirsk, 'The European Debate on Customs of Inheritance 1500–1700', in J. Goody, J. Thirsk and E.P Thompson (eds), *Family and Inheritance*, Cambridge, Cambridge University Press, 1976, p. 183.

26 Thirsk, ibid., p. 191.

27 Pollock and Maitland, Vol. II, op. cit., p. 264.

28 For example, S. Firestone, *The Dialectic of Sex*, London, The Women's Press, 1979.

29 Pollock and Maitland, Vol. II, op. cit., p. 265; see P. Anderson, *Passages from Antiquity to Feudalism*, London, New Left Books,

1974, for a discussion of the parcelisation of sovereignty under feudalism.

30 Pollock and Maitland, Vol. II, op. cit., p. 264.

31 W. Holdsworth, *A History of English Law*, Vol. III (third edition), London, Methuen, 1923, p. 55.

32 C. Creighton, 'Family Property and Relations of Production in Western Europe', *Economy and Society*, 9 (2), 1980, p. 146.

33 C. Hill, *Reformation to Industrial Revolution*, Harmondsworth, Penguin, 1969, p. 147. By entailing estates landowners were able to legally restrict the transmission of estates to a specified line of heirs. The practice was designed to protect and preserve the principle of primogeniture and thus the preservation and accumulation of property (L. Stone, *The Family, Sex and Marriage in England 1500–1800*, London, Weidenfeld and Nicolson, 1977, p. 87). However, from about the middle of the seventh century, trustees to preserve contingent remainders facilitated the protection of the interests of the unborn son of the marriage.

To elaborate: typically an entailed estate would be conveyed to Lord A for life, then to his son B for life, with the remainder in tail to B's eldest son, and similar remainders in tail to B's younger children. B would thus be unable to get full powers of alienation over the estate as a limitation in favour of trustees was part of the settlement. The trustees were 'to preserve the interests of B's unborn sons', i.e. the contingent remainders. Before B's son became the tenant in tail and thus able to alienate the estate, the estate would normally be resettled by agreement by B and his son. B would continue as life tenant in remainder to B's son. The remainder would be intact to B's grandson (G.E. Mingay, *English Landed Society in the Eighteenth Century*, London, Routledge & Kegan Paul, 1963, pp. 72–73; J. Habakkuk, 'Marriage Settlements in the Eighteenth Century', *Transactions of the Royal Historical Society* (fourth series), 32, 1950; C. Clay, 'Marriage, Inheritance, and the Rise of Large Estates in England, 1660–1815,' *Economic History Review* (2nd series), 21, 1968; L. Bonfield, 'Marriage Settlements and the Rise of Great Estates: The Demographic Aspect', *Economic History Review*, 32, 1979). As only a life tenant, the eldest son was not able to override provision for his younger brothers and sisters (Habakkuk, op. cit., p. 17). By the early eighteenth century, this form of strict settlement was the usual way of settling estates and provided for children among landowning families (ibid., p. 18).

34 Thirsk, 1976, op. cit., p. 183.

35 Quoted in ibid., p. 184.

36 F. M. L. Thompson, *English Landed Society in the Nineteenth Century*, London, Routledge & Kegan Paul, 1963, p. 65.

37 Hill, 1969, op. cit., pp. 146–147.

38 Thompson, op. cit., p. 69.

39 J. P. Cooper, 'Inheritance and Settlement by Great Landowners', in Goody, Thirsk and Thompson, op. cit., p. 195.

40 Thirsk, 1976, op. cit., p. 186.

41 Ibid., p. 184.
42 Ibid., p. 188.
43 R. Trumbach, *The Rise of the Egalitarian Family*, London, Academic Press, 1978, p. 72.
44 Thirsk, 1964, op. cit., p. 12.
45 Ibid.
46 Ibid., p. 118.
47 R. Faith, 'Peasant Families and Inheritance Customs in Medieval England', *Agricultural History Review*, 14, 1966–7, pp. 14–15.
48 Ibid., pp. 85–86.
49 Ibid., p. 86.
50 J. Goody, 'Inheritance, Property and Marriage in Africa and Eurasia', *Sociology*, 3, 1969, pp. 55–76; Pollock and Maitland, Vol. II, op. cit., pp. 260–261.
51 J. Goody, *Production and Reproduction*, London, Cambridge University Press, 1976, p. 6.
52 Muller, op. cit., p. 17.
53 Fell, op. cit., p. 16.
54 Muller, op. cit., p. 17.
55 Goody, 1976, op. cit., p. 7.
56 G. Lerner, *The Creation of Patriarchy*, Oxford, Oxford University Press, 1986, p. 108.
57 G. Homans, *English Villagers of the Thirteenth Century*, Cambridge, MA: Harvard University Press, 1941, pp. 133–134.
58 C. B. Macpherson, 'Capitalism and the Changing Concept of Property', in E. Kemenka and R.S. Neale (eds), *Feudalism, Capitalism and Beyond*, Canberra, Australian National University Press, 1975, pp. 108–110.
59 R. S. Neale, 'The Bourgeois Historically has Played a Most Revolutionary Part', in Kamenka and Neale, op. cit., p. 96.
60 Fell, op. cit., p. 59.
61 C. S. Kenny, *The History of England as to the Effects of Marriage on Property and on the Wives Legal Capacity*, London, Reeves Turner, 1879, p. 43; F.G. Buckstaff, 'Married Women's Property in Anglo-Saxon and Anglo-Norman Law and the Origin of Common Law Dower', *American Academy of Political and Social Science Annals*, 4, 1893, p. 50.
62 Fell, op. cit., p. 57; Meyer, op.cit., p. 63; Buckstaff, op. cit., pp. 44- 49.
63 Fell, op. cit., p. 59.
64 Ibid., p. 76.
65 Meyer, op. cit., p. 62.
66 P. Wormald, 'Warrior Women', *London Review of Books*, 19 June 1986.
67 T. Anstey, *The Lawes Resolutions of Women's Rights*, London, John More, 1632, pp. 129–130 and quoted in R. Thompson, *Women in Stuart England and America*, London, Routledge & Kegan Paul, 1974, p. 162.
68 Holdsworth, Vol. III, op. cit., p. 525.
69 Ibid., pp. 523–527.

70 J. H. Baker, *An Introduction to English Legal History* (second edition), London, Butterworths, 1979, p. 396.
71 Kenny, op. cit., pp. 76–77.
72 Ibid., p. 395.
73 Ibid., p. 398.
74 J. Goody, *The Development of the Family and Marriage in Europe*, London, Cambridge University Press, 1983, pp. 256–258.
75 Habakkuk, op.cit., pp. 26–30.
76 E. Mason, 'Moritagium and the Changing Law', *Bulletin of the Institute of Historical Research*, 49, 1976.
77 L. Stone, *The Crisis of the Aristocracy 1558–1641*, London, Oxford University Press, 1965, p. 633.
78 For example, Homans, op. cit., p. 141.
79 Stone, 1965, op. cit., pp. 637–642.
80 Habakkuk, op. cit., pp. 26–30; Mingay, op. cit. See also Clay, op. cit.
81 Klink, op. cit., p. 117.
82 See, for example, the 'Kentish Betrothal' quoted in Kenny, op. cit., p. 26. Patrick Wormald suggests that variations with respect to the size of the widow's dower may well represent geographical variation rather than chronological change (personal communication, 1987).
83 Holdsworth, op. cit., p. 193; Thorne, op. cit., pp. 265, 268.
84 Hall, op. cit., pp. 59–60.
85 Pollock and Maitland, Vol. III, op. cit., p. 421.
86 R. H.Hilton, *The English Peasantry in the Late Middle Ages*, Oxford, Clarendon Press, 1975, p. 79.
87 Ibid., p. 100.
88 E. Coke, *A Commentary on Littleton*, Vol. I, Chapter 5, section 37 (18th edition) J. & S. Brooke, 1823.
89 R. A. Houlbrooke, *The English Family 1450–1700*, Essex, Longman, 1984, p. 210.
90 Macpherson, op. cit., p. 105.
91 Ibid., p. 110.
92 M. Bloch, *Feudal Society* Vol I (trans. L. A. Manyon), London, Routledge & Kegan Paul, 1965, pp. 115–116.
93 A. Macfarlane, *The Origins of English Individualism*, Oxford, Basil Blackwell, 1978, p. 103.
94 Ibid., p. 106.
95 Ibid., pp. 195–196.
96 Ibid., p. 206.
97 Ibid., pp. 106, 170.
98 K. Marx (1857–8), *Grundrisse*, Harmondsworth, Penguin, 1973.
99 R. Hilton, *The Transition from Feudalism to Capitalism*, London, Verso, 1978, pp. 25–26.
100 Ibid., p. 30.
101 Macpherson, op. cit., p. 109.
102 Ibid., pp. 105–107.
103 P. Zagorin, *The Court and the Country*, London, Routledge & Kegan Paul, 1969, discussed in P. Corrigan and D. Sayer, *The Great Arch*, Oxford, Blackwell, 1985, p. 73.

104 Quoted in G. Aylmer, 'The Meaning and Definition of Property in Seventeenth Century England', *Past and Present*, 86, 1980, p. 89.
105 Quoted in ibid., p. 92.
106 Quoted in ibid., p. 93.
107 Quoted in ibid., p. 102.
108 K. Thomas, 'Women and the Civil War Sects', *Past and Present*, 13, 1958, p. 55; J. Thirsk, 'Younger Sons in the Seventeenth Century', *History*, 54, 1969, pp. 376–377; Thirsk, 1976, op. cit., pp. 186–187.
109 R. Harrison and F. Mort, 'Patriarchal Aspects of Nineteenth-Century State Formation', in P. Corrigan (ed.), *Capitalism, State Formation and Marxist Theory*, London, Quartet Books, 1980, pp. 85–86.
110 J. Humphries, 'Class Struggle and the Persistence of the Working-Class Family', *Cambridge Journal of Economics*, 13, 1977.
111 M. Barrett and M. McIntosh, 'The Family Wage: Some Problems for Socialists and Feminists', *Capital and Class*, 11, 1980.
112 J. Brenner and M. Ramas, 'Rethinking Women's Oppression', *New Left Review*, 144, 1984.
113 Baker, op. cit., pp. 397–398.
114 R. Thompson, op. cit., p. 163; Kenny, op. cit., pp. 99–101; Sir William Holdsworth, *A History of English Law*, Vol. V, London, Methuen, 1924, pp. 311–315; J. Greenberge, 'The Legal Status of the English Woman in Early Eighteenth Century Common Law and Equity', *Studies in Eighteenth Century Culture*, 4, 1975.

5 FROM 'THE LAW OF THE FATHER' TO 'CAPITALIST FRATERNITY'

1 In Lacanian theory the Oedipal crisis represents entry into the Symbolic Order, an entry which is also bound up with the acquisition of language. In the Oedipal crisis the father splits the unity between mother and child. The phallus, which represents the Law of the Father (or the threat of castration) signifies loss and separation to the child. Desire for the mother or an imaginary unity with the mother is repressed. Useful introductions to Lacan include; T. Moi, *Sexual/Textual Politics*, London, Methuen, 1985, pp. 99–101; and E. Grosz, *Jacques Lacan: A Feminist Introduction*, London, Routledge, 1990.
2 C. Pateman, *The Disorder of Women*, Cambridge, Polity Press, 1989, Chapter 2. See also P. Laslett (ed.), *Patriarcha and Other Political Works*, Oxford, Blackwell, 1949.
3 Laslett, ibid., pp. 21–22.
4 Laslett, ibid., pp. 13–20.
5 C. Pateman, *The Sexual Contract*, Cambridge: Polity Press, 1988, p.x.
6 Pateman, 1989, op. cit., p. 38.
7 Ibid.
8 Ibid.

9 S. Bassett, 'In Search of the Origins of Anglo-Saxon Kingdoms', in S. Bassett (ed.), *The Origins Of Anglo-Saxon Kingdoms*, London, Leicester University Press, 1989, p. 23.

10 Ibid.

11 Ibid. Other material on Anglo-Saxon state formation includes J. Campbell, 'Observations on English Government from the Tenth to the Twelfth Centuries', *Transactions of the Royal Historical Society* (5th series) vol. 25; J. Campbell (ed.), *The Anglo-Saxons*, Phaidon Press, Oxford, 1982; P. Corrigan and D. Sayer, *The Great Arch*, Basil Blackwell, Oxford, 1985, Chapter 1.

12 Laslett, op. cit., pp. 12–13.

13 V. Muller, 'The Formation of the State and the Oppression of Women: Some Theoretical Considerations and a Case Study in England and Wales', *Review of Radical Political Economy*, 9, 1977, p. 16.

14 See, e.g., M. Bloch, *Feudal Society* Vol I, London, Routledge & Kegan Paul, 1962, p. 167.

15 Ibid., p. 148.

16 Ibid., p. 147.

17 Ibid., p. 200, Lucas, op. cit., p. 201.

18 Pateman, 1989, op. cit., p. 50.

19 Quoted in ibid. p. 50.

20 Bloch, op. cit., p. 201; Lucas, op. cit., p. 84.

21 J. Kelly-Gadol, 'Did Women Have a Renaissance?' in R. Bridenthal and C. Koonz (eds), *Becoming Visible: Women in European History*, Boston, Houghton Mifflin, 1977, p. 145.

22 C. Fell, *Women in Anglo-Saxon England*, Bloomington, Indiana State University Press, 1984, p. 99.

23 Bloch, op. cit., p. 200.

24 Kelly-Gadol, op. cit., p. 145.

25 See e.g. P. Hogrefe, *Tudor Women: Commoners and Queens*, Iowa State University Press, 1975, Chapter 6 'Women as Manor Wives . . .'

26 A. Clarke, *Working Life of Women in the Seventeenth Century*, London, Routledge & Kegan Paul, 1982, Chapter V.

27 B. S. Anderson and J. P. Zinsser, *A History of Their Own*, Vol. I, London, Penguin, 1988, p. 373.

28 R. Hilton, *The English Peasantry in the Late Middle Ages*, Oxford, Clarendon Press, 1975, pp. 95–110.

29 M. Stopes, *British Freewomen*, London, Simon Sonnenschein, 1907, p. 85.

30 P. Corrigan and D. Sayer, op. cit., p. 21.

31 Ibid., p. 39.

32 There were some isolated instances of women holding offices of Sheriff and Justice of the Peace. See M. Stopes, op. cit., pp. 53, 63; A. Chapman, *The Status of Women under English Law*, New York, Dutton & Co., 1909, p. 12.

33 According to F. Pollock and W. Maitland, *History of English Law Before the Time of Edward I*, Vol. I, Cambridge, Cambridge University Press, 1898, p. 484, the only time that women ever sat as jurors

in the temporal courts was in cases where an expectant heir alleged
he was being displaced by a suppositious child.

34 P. Stafford, *Queens, Concubines and Dowagers: The King's Wife in
the Early Middle Ages*, Athens, The University of Georgia Press,
1983, p. 195.
35 Muller, op. cit., p. 13.
36 Corrigan and Sayer, op. cit., p. 39.
37 F. W. Maitland, *The Constitutional History of England*, Cambridge,
Cambridge University Press, 1908, p. 209.
38 J. H. Baker, *An Introduction to English Legal History* (second
edition) Butterworth, 1979, p. 27, Quoted in Corrigan and Sayer op.
cit., p. 31.
39 Corrigan and Sayer, op. cit., p. 31. For a comparison of the English
situation with other European politics, see P. Anderson, *Lineages of
the Absolutist State*, London, New Left Books, 1974.
40 Anderson, ibid., pp. 115–116.
41 See discussion in Corrigan and Sayer, op. cit., and Anderson, op. cit.
42 Corrigan and Sayer, op. cit.
43 J. C. Holt, *Magna Carta*, London, Cambridge University Press, 1965,
p. 327.
44 Laslett, op. cit., p. 19.
45 Anderson, op. cit., p. 113.
46 Ibid. p. 113.
47 Ibid. p. 114.
48 Ibid. p. 119; Corrigan and Sayer, op. cit., p. 43.
49 Anderson, op. cit., p. 119.
50 D. Loades, *Politics and the Nation 1450–1660*, London, Fontana,
1977, p. 175.
51 Corrigan and Sayer, op. cit., p. 46. Before the Norman Conquest
temporal and ecclesiastical jurisdictions were not separated. In 1072
they were separated by William I. From that time the ecclesiastical
courts administered Canon Law. By the early fourteenth century the
church had jurisdiction over marriage and illegitimacy, succession to
personal property and punishment of mortal sins such as fornication
and adultery. The ecclesiastical courts also dealt with slander until
the sixteenth century. Clearly, then, church law impacted on the
lives of most of the English population. See Corrigan and Sayer,
op. cit., p. 40 for these points.
52 A. Myers, *England in the Late Middle Ages*, Harmondsworth, Penguin, 1952, pp. 193–194.
53 Corrigan and Sayer, op. cit., p. 25.
54 Anderson, op. cit., p. 118.
55 Ibid., p. 120.
56 Ibid., pp. 121–122.
57 Ibid., p. 115.
58 Corrigan and Sayer, op. cit.
59 Anderson, op. cit., p. 114.
60 Ibid., p. 114.
61 Corrigan and Sayer, op. cit., p. 29.

62 Anderson, op. cit., p. 115.
63 Ibid., p. 119.
64 Myers, op. cit., p. 199.
65 Corrigan and Sayer, op. cit., p. 51.
66 Quoted in Corrigan and Sayer, op. cit., p. 25.
67 Ibid., p. 29.
68 Stopes, op. cit., pp. 68–69.
69 Chapman, op. cit., p. 1.
70 Stopes, op. cit., pp. 116–117.
71 Chapman, op. cit., p. 30.
72 Stopes, op. cit., p. 118.
73 Laslett, op. cit., p. 12.
74 Stafford, op. cit., pp. 194–195.
75 S. Coontz and P. Henderson (eds), *Women's Work, Men's Property*, London, Verso, 1986, pp. 146–147.
76 Corrigan and Sayer, op. cit., e.g. pp. 46, 60, 61.
77 S. Basnett, *Elizabeth I*, Oxford, Berg, 1988, p. 94.
78 See discussion in A. Heisch, 'Queen Elizabeth I and the Persistence of Patriarchy', *Feminist Review*, 4, 1980.
79 Quoted in Heisch, op. cit., p. 53.
80 Quoted in ibid., p. 52.
81 Ibid., p. 53.
82 Ibid., p. 47.
83 Anderson, op. cit., p. 125.
84 Pateman, 1989, op. cit., p. 42.
85 J. Lewis, *Women in England 1870–1950*, Sussex, Wheatsheaf, 1984, p.x.
86 Chapman, op. cit., p. 32.
87 Sir E. Coke, *Institute of the Laws of England* (fourth part), London, J. Flescher, for W. Lee and D. Packman, 1660.
88 Chapman, op. cit., p. 37.
89 Ibid., pp. 35–36, Stopes, op. cit., pp. 151–6.
90 Chapman, op. cit., p. 36.
91 K. Van Der Steinten, 'The Discovery of Women in Eighteenth-Century English Political Life', in B. Kanner (ed.), *The Women of England From Anglo-Saxon Times to the Present*, London, Mansell, 1980.
92 Quoted in C. B. Macpherson, *The Political Theory of Possessive Individualism*, Oxford, Clarendon Press, 1962, p. 296, note 1.
93 E. A. McArthur, 'Women Petitioners and the Long Parliament', *English Historical Review*, 24, 1909, p. 709; Macpherson, op. cit., p. 296.
94 C. Hill, *Winstanley: The Law of Freedom and Other Writings*, Cambridge, Cambridge University Press, 1983.
95 Ibid., p. 464. For women's participation in the Civil War Sects and political activity generally during the seventeenth century, see e.g. K. Thomas, 'Women and the Civil War Sects', *Past and Present*, 13, 1958; D. Weigall, 'Women Militants in the English Civil War',

History Today, 22, 1972; E. M. Williams, 'Women Preachers in the Civil War', *Journal of Modern History*, vol. 1, 1929.
96 D. Leonard Barker, 'Regulation of Marriage', in G. Littlejohn et al. (eds), *Power and the State*, London, Croom Helm, 1978, p. 256.
97 Pateman, 1989, op. cit., pp. 44–47.
98 See e.g. Corrigan and Sayer, op. cit., pp. 72–77.
99 D. Hirst, *The Representatives of the People?* London, Cambridge University Press, 1975, p. 18.
100 Quoted in Stopes, op. cit., pp. 130–131.
101 Stone, *Social Change and Revolution in England, 1540–1640*, Longman, 1965, p. 38, quoted in Corrigan and Sayer, op. cit., p. 74.
102 S. F. C. Milsom, *Studies in the History of the Common Law*, London, Hambledon, 1985, p. 199.
103 Ibid., p. 201.
104 Ibid., p. 200.
105 C. Hill, 'A Bourgeois Revolution?' in J. Pocock (ed.), *Three British Revolutions*, Princeton, Princeton University Press, 1980, p. 118.
106 C. Hill, *Intellectual Origins of the English Revolution*, Oxford, Clarendon, 1965, p. 250.
107 Chapman, op. cit., p. 37.
108 Macpherson, op. cit., p. 296.
109 Ibid.
110 Ibid.
111 Barker, op. cit., p. 256.
112 Hill, 1983, op. cit., p. 465.
113 Ibid.
114 Pateman, 1989, op. cit., pp. 39–40.
115 M. Butler, 'Early Liberal Roots of Feminism: John Locke and the Attack on Patriarchy', in M. Lyndon Shanley and C. Pateman (eds), *Feminist Interpretations and Political Theory*, Cambridge, Polity, 1991, p. 88.
116 Ibid., p. 89 n 51.
117 Ibid., p. 88.
118 Pateman, 1988, op. cit., p. 21.
119 Ibid., p. 52.
120 Quoted in ibid.
121 M. Brody, 'Mary Wollstonecraft – Sexuality and Women's Rights', in D. Spender, *Feminist Theorists*, London, The Women's Press, 1983, p. 44.
122 D. Spender, *Women of Ideas*, London, Arc, p. 147.
123 Quoted in Pateman, 1988, op. cit., p. 53.
124 Pateman, 1989, op. cit., p. 121.
125 Laslett, op. cit., pp. 11–20.
126 Quoted in C. Pateman, ' "God Hath Ordained to Man a Helper": Hobbes, Patriarchy and Conjugal Right', in Stanley and Pateman, op. cit., p. 63.
127 Quoted in ibid., p. 63.
128 R. W. K. Hilton, 'Husbands, Fathers and Conquerors', *Political Studies*, vol. 16, 1968, p. 57.

129 See discussion in ibid.
130 Quoted in D. Sayer, *The Violence of Abstraction*, Oxford, Blackwell, 1987, p. 100.
131 Ibid. p. 100.
132 K. Marx, (1843), 'On The Jewish Question' p. 154. Quoted in Sayer, op. cit., pp. 103–104.

6 SISTERS, DAUGHTERS AND SUBORDINATE WIVES

1 K. Sacks, *Sisters and Wives*, London, Greenwood Press, 1979, p. 123.
2 A. L. Klinck, 'Anglo-Saxon Women and the Law', *Journal of Medieval History*, 8, 1982, p. 111.
3 V. Muller, 'The Formation of the State and the Oppression of Women: Some Theoretical Considerations and a Case Study in England and Wales', *Review of Radical Political Economy*, 9, 1977, p. 16.
4 Klinck, op. cit., p. 112.
5 Ibid.
6 L. Lancaster, 'Kinship In Anglo-Saxon Society – 1', *British Journal of Sociology*, 9, 1958, p. 245.
7 C. Fell, *Women in Anglo-Saxon England*, Oxford, Blackwell, 1986, p. 74.
8 F. L. Attenborough (ed.), *The Laws of the Earliest English Kings*, Cambridge, Cambridge University Press, 1922, pp. 55, 57.
9 Klink, op. cit., p. 112.
10 Quoted in Fell, op. cit., p. 59.
11 Lancaster, op. cit., p. 245.
12 Quoted in Fell, op. cit., p. 59.
13 Klink, op. cit., p. 111.
14 A. J. Robertson (ed. and trans.) *The Laws of the Kings of England from Edmund to Henry*, London, Cambridge University Press, 1925, p. 213.
15 Ibid. p. 85.
16 Fell, op. cit.
17 Attenborough, op. cit., pp. 55, 57.
18 T. M. Charles Edwards, 'Kinship, Status and the Origins of the Hide', *Past and Present*, 56, 1972, p. 10.
19 Robertson , op. cit., p. 215.
20 Sacks, op. cit., pp. 122–123.
21 Lancaster, op. cit., p. 232 and II, p. 359.
22 Ibid. II, p. 359.
23 Lancaster I, op. cit., p. 239.
24 Lancaster II, op. cit., p. 372.
25 Ibid. p. 373.
26 Ibid. p. 373.
27 Lancaster I, op. cit., p. 239.
28 Lancaster II, op. cit., p. 372.
29 Ibid.

30 J. Goody, *Production and Reproduction*, Cambridge, Cambridge University Press, 1976, p. 103.
31 J. Bennett, *Women in the Medieval English Countryside*, Oxford, Oxford University Press, 1987, p. 108. See also R. Kittel, 'Women under the Law in Medieval England 1066–1488', in B. Kanner (ed.), *The Women of England from Anglo-Saxon Times to the Present*, London, Mansell, 1980.
32 J. H. Baker, *An Introduction to English Legal History*, (second edition), London, Butterworths, 1979, p. 395.
33 *Statutes of the Realm*, Vol. I, London, 1829–63, Parliament, p. 320.
34 Baker, op. cit., p. 428.
35 P. Corrigan and D. Sayer, *The Great Arch*, Oxford, Blackwell, 1985, p. 36.
36 Sir W. Blackstone, *Commentaries on the Law of England*, (ninth edition), Oxford Streatham, Cadell & Prince, 1783, pp. 444–5. T. Anstey *The Lawes Resolution of Women's Rights*, London, John More, 1632, p. 128.
37 S. Coontz and P. Henderson, 'Property Forms, Political Power and Female Labour in the Origins of Class and State Societies', in S. Coontz and P. Henderson (eds) *Women's Work, Men's Property*, London, Verso, p. 152.
38 P. Wormald, Personal Communication, 1987.
39 D. Loades, *Politics and the Nation 1450–1660*, London, Fontana, 1977, p. 175; quoted in Corrigan and Sayer, op. cit., p. 45.
40 A. Myers, *England in the Late Middle Ages*, Harmondsworth, Penguin, 1952, pp. 193–194.
41 C. Hill, *Society and Puritanism in Pre-Revolutionary England*, London, Secker & Warburg, 1964, p. 446.
42 Corrigan and Sayer, op. cit., p. 46.
43 Hill, op. cit., p. 447.
44 A. Macfarlane, *Marriage and Love in England 1300–1840*, Oxford, Blackwell, 1986, p. 287.
45 For example, C. Pateman, *The Sexual Contract*, Cambridge, Polity Press, 1988, p. 119.
46 Macfarlane, op. cit., p. 287.
47 E. Z. Wiener, 'Is a Spinster an Unmarried Woman?' *American Journal of Legal History*, 20, 1976, p. 28.
48 R. Kittel, 'Women under the Law in Medieval England 1066–1485', in Kanner, op. cit., pp. 129–130.
49 Blackstone, op. cit., p. 444.
50 T. E. (possibly Edwards) op. cit., p. 128.
51 J. Bennett, *Women in the Medieval English Countryside*, Oxford, Oxford University Press, 1987, Chapter 5.
52 Fell, op. cit., pp. 149–150; L. Stone, *The Family, Sex and Marriage in England, 1500–1800*, London, Weidenfield and Nicolson, Chapter 7.
53 Fell, op. cit., pp. 150–151.
54 G. Homans, *English Villagers of the Thirteenth Century*, Cambridge MA, Harvard University Press, pp. 160–163.
55 C. Middleton, 'Peasants, Patriarchy and the Feudal Mode of Pro-

duction in England: A Marxist Appraisal II', *Sociological Review,* 29, 1981.
56 Ibid.
57 L. Stone, *The Crisis of the Aristocracy 1558–1641,* London, Oxford University Press, 1965, pp. 605–609.
58 F. Pollock and W. Maitland, *History of English Law before the Time of Edward I,* Vol. I, Cambridge, Cambridge University Press, 1898, pp. 328–329.
59 M. J. Hawkins, 'Royal Wardship in the Seventeenth Century,' *The Genealogists Magazine,* 16(2), 1969; J. Hurstfield 'Wardship and Marriage under Elizabeth I', *History Today,* 4(9), 1954; Stone, 1965, op. cit., pp. 600–605.
60 C. Hill, *Reformation to Industrial Revolution,* Middlesex, Pelican, 1969, p. 146.
61 Hawkins, op. cit., p. 45; Stone, op. cit., pp. 604–605.
62 L. Stone, *The Family, Sex and Marriage in England 1500–1800,* London, Weidenfield & Nicolson, 1977, p. 272.
63 Ibid., pp. 279–280.
64 C. Hill *Puritanism and Revolution,* London, Secker & Warburg, 1958, p. 373.
65 Ibid., pp. 383–384.
66 Stone, 1977, op. cit., pp. 315–316.
67 Macfarlane, op. cit., p. 214; Stone, 1977, op. cit., pp. 292–297.
68 Stone, 1977, op. cit., pp. 213–214.
69 R. Trumbach, *The Rise of the Egalitarian Family,* London, Academic Press, 1978, p. 109.
70 Ibid., pp. 97–102.
71 J. Sarsby, *Romantic Love and Society,* Middlesex, Penguin, 1983, p. 47.
72 Ibid., p. 52.

7 WOMEN AS PROPERTY

1 A. J. Robertson (ed. and trans.), *The Laws of the Kings of England from Edmund to Henry,* London, Cambridge University Press, 1925, p. 203.
2 F. L. Attenborough (ed.), *The Laws of the Earliest English Kings,* Cambridge, Cambridge University Press, 1922, p. 71.
3 N. Basher, 'Rape in England between 1550 and 1700' in London Feminist History Group, *The Sexual Dynamics of History,* London, Pluto Press, 1983, p. 30.
4 Attenborough, op. cit., pp. 5–7.
5 A. L. Klink, 'Anglo-Saxon Women and the Law', *Journal of Medieval History,* 8, 1982, p. 109. Klink assumes that Aethelbert was legislating for cases of rape, but it is unclear from his language whether he intended to take the woman's side into account. If she was a willing party to the sexual act, he may have considered that a crime had nonetheless been committed, against her guardian or master.

6 Basher, op. cit., p. 30.
7 See discussion in ibid., and also J. B. Post 'Ravishment of Women and the Statutes of Westminster', in J. H. Baker (ed.), *Legal Records and the Historian*, Cambridge, Cambridge University Press, 1978; and E. W. Ives, 'Agaynst Taking Awaye of Women: The Inception and Operation of the Abduction Act of 1487', in E. W. Ives, R. J. Knecht and J. J. Scarisbrick (eds), *Wealth and Power in Tudor England*, London, Athlone, 1978.
8 F. Engels, 'The Origins of the Family, Private Property and the State', in K. Marx and F. Engels, *Selected Works*, London, Lawrence & Wishart, 1968.
9 Quoted in L. Lancaster 'Kinship in Anglo-Saxon Society I', *British Journal of Sociology*, 9, 1958, p. 246.
10 C. Fell, *Women in Anglo-Saxon England*, Oxford, Blackwell, 1986, pp. 71–73.
11 Ibid., p. 20.
12 P. Wormald, 'Warrior Women', *London Review of Books*, 19 June 1986.
13 Robertson, op. cit., p. 95.
14 Quoted in Lancaster, op. cit., p. 244.
15 F. Pollock and W. Maitland, *History of English Law before the Time of Edward I*, Vol. II, Cambridge, Cambridge University Press, 1898, pp. 367–369. See also pp. 365–366 for the role of the ecclesiastical courts in deciding whether or not there had been a marriage.
16 Ibid. p. 368.
17 C. Middleton, 'Peasants, Patriarchy and the Feudal Mode of Production in England: A Marxist Appraisal I', *Sociological Review*, 29, 1981, p. 114.
18 Quoted in P. Corrigan and D. Sayer, *The Great Arch*, Oxford, Blackwell, 1985, p. 50.
19 O. R. McGregor, *Divorce In England*, London, Heinemann, 1957, p. 14.
20 Middleton, ibid., II, pp. 144–145.
21 Ibid., pp. 143.
22 Ibid., pp. 145–146.
23 Ibid., p. 151.
24 Ibid.
25 Fell, op. cit., p. 59, citing Aethelbert 77, that a marriage contract would stand if there had been no dishonesty, but if that deception had occurred, e.g. if a husband found himself supporting another man's child, the bridegroom would receive back the money he had paid to the bride.
26 Attenborough, op. cit., p. 73.
27 See e.g. Aethelred, law 26.1 in Robertson, op.cit., p. 99.
28 Attenborough, op. cit., p. 71.
29 See discussion in Fell, op. cit., pp. 20, 71–73; Wormald, op. cit. J. Goody in *The Development of the Family and Marriage in Europe*, Cambridge, Cambridge University Press, 1983, has discussed the

suppression of concubinage by the Christian church in the German lands, pp. 76–77.

30 V. Muller, 'The Formation of the State and the Oppression of Women: Some Theoretical Considerations and a Case Study in England and Wales', *Review of Radical Political Economy*, 9, 1977, p. 8.

31 Goody, op. cit., p. 4.

32 Ibid., p. 42.

33 Ibid., p. 77.

34 Lancaster, op. cit., p. 241.

35 Robertson, op. cit., p. 95.

36 Ibid., p. 201.

37 Attenborough, op. cit., p. 105.

38 Goody, op. cit., pp. 43–44.

39 Ibid., p. 57.

40 Ibid., p. 59.

41 Attenborough, op. cit., p. 15.

42 J. Thrupp, *The Anglo-Saxon Home*, London, Longman, Green, Longman & Roberts, 1862, p. 64.

43 Goody, op. cit., p. 44.

44 Ibid., p. 46.

45 Quoted in G. E. Howard, *A History of Matrimonial Institutions*, Chicago, University of Chicago Press, 1904, p. 40.

46 Quoted in ibid., p. 40.

47 Ibid., pp. 40–41.

48 G. Lerner, *The Creation of Patriarchy*, Oxford, Oxford University Press, 1986, pp. 213–214.

49 Ibid., p. 213.

50 A. Whitehead, 'Women and Men; Kinship and Property: Some General Issues [1]', in R. Hirschon (ed.), *Women and Property – Women as Property*, London, Croom Helm, p. 180.

51 M. Strathern, 'Subject or Object? Women and the Circulation of Valuables in Highland New Guinea (1)', in Hirschon, op. cit., p. 164.

52 Strathern, op. cit., p. 165.

53 Ibid.

54 Ibid.

55 Ibid., pp. 167–168.

56 Attenborough, op. cit., p. 85.

57 Basher, op. cit., p. 41.

58 Ibid., p. 40.

59 Quoted in Hirschon, op. cit., p. 180.

60 Basher, op. cit., p. 32.

61 See e.g. L. Stone, *The Family, Sex and Marriage in England 1500–1800*, London, Weidenfield & Nicolson, 1977; *The Crisis of the Aristocracy, 1558–1641*, London, Oxford University Press, 1965; G. Homans, *English Villagers of the Thirteenth Century*, Cambridge, MA, Harvard University Press, 1941, pp. 160–163; Fell, op. cit., pp. 150–153.

62 J. Goody, *Production and Reproduction*, Cambridge, Cambridge University Press, 1976, p. 106.
63 Ibid., p. 103.
64 Basher, op. cit., p. 40.

CONCLUSION

1 J. Thirsk, 'Younger Sons in the Seventeenth Century', *History*, 54, 1969, pp. 376–377.
2 See e.g. M. Barrett, *Women's Oppression Today*, London, Verso, 1988, Introduction.
3 I would also argue that age and ethnicity can be expressions of the social relation of property and that age and ethnicity can similarly constitute the social relation of property. Indeed, the social division of age has been implicit in some of my discussion of inheritance practices. It was discussed in campaigns against primogeniture and entails in the sixteenth and seventeenth centuries (see Thirsk, op. cit. and K. Thomas, 'Women and the Civil War Sects', *Past and Present*, 13, 1958). Sociological texts on the political economy of racism and labour migration are founded upon an understanding of racism and ethnicity in relation to property. See e.g. R. Miles and A. Phizacklea, *White Man's Country*, London, Pluto, 1984; S. Castles and G. Kosack, *Immigrant Workers and Class Structure in Western Europe*, London, Oxford University Press, 1973.
4 S. Bassett, 'In Search of the Origins of Anglo-Saxon Kingdoms', in S. Bassett (ed.), *The Origins of Anglo-Saxon Kingdoms*, London, Leicester University Press, 1989, p. 23.
5 Quoted in D. Sayer, *The Violence of Abstraction*, Oxford, Blackwell, 1987, p. 100.
6 Quoted in ibid., p. 100.
7 E. P. Thompson, *The Poverty of Theory*, London, Merlin, 1978, e.g. p. 288.
8 Ibid.

Index